Orbs of
Illuminations

ORB TRILOGY

Orbs of Illuminations

Aurora of Spirit

IRIS SANKOH-DOUGLAS

THE CHOIR PRESS

First published in the United Kingdom in 2023 by
The Choir Press

ISBN 978-1-78963-398-6

Orb's Note

Redefining this journey is where individuals appear and disappear into and throughout my mind landscapes. I am that constant. It is I who am that visitor. One who calls upon, makes known of, becomes an acquaintance to those who have come to visit me. A weathered traveller of endless universes, replete with stories, dusted with eccentricities and entities too strange for anything but quiet times, laced with fondant-fancied memories of how life could be, if so wished.

This journey I travel with my two incredible daughters. They are given to me to replace every breath. I do realise this miracle.

Without need of taking, they are eternal wealth. Without wanting, they are contentment. Without ego, they are infinite. Without fear, they are Love. They teach me whatever I need to understand in this lifetime, then some. My girls remind me what it is I am Here for, as well as allow me to evolve within their lights. They are my Universe where infinite worlds await us.

My gratitude and forever friends; my personal throng of learned Angels; David Onyett, Rachel Woodman and Adrian Sysum of The Choir Press.

In this meeting of minds, I have learnt the art of creativity is a process to be shared, with best friends, loud laughter, exchanges of fantastical daydreams, and a constant sprinkling of belief in pure magic waiting to be invited through the kaleidoscope of understanding how life is not just a series of randomness. As you see, our meeting has been to share, from here on, something inexplicable.

Throughout each journey I encounter their knowledge hidden within psychological support.

I not only absorb their invaluable knowledge but am actively tutored in this art of writing for publication. We shall travel endless journeys together, my wonderful wizards of words and all things worldly. It is they who have taught me to speak with a voice of clarity grown from confidence they instil in me.

It is they who have discovered how to translate my language and understand its meaning, as much as humanly possible. The ultimate proof of their achieving this, lies within the pages of these two unusual and extremely eccentric works. The Choir Press is this uniqueness that rescues my sanity but accepts my insanity with humour and I am humbled by such integrity. Without all these elements of all our lives, we are unable to achieve meaning, a sense of what community creativeness is. This life is the root system for our tree of existence. Our survival depends upon all our abilities, all our strengths. Most importantly, our Oneness of compassion, which when it comes down to our nth degree, will be our universal language of communication and connectiveness.

Orb's trilogy is an active address to this sacredness of this life. To hold up my light of consciousness, a capturing of positive elements, and those far beyond this world's perceptions. Orb is on Her journeys of discovering what humans can create within themselves, that are catalysts to existence, the connection of existences, able to achieve Universal Oneness in order to evolve into our Sacred Selves.

Iris's Note

This is a minute drop of sacredness I administer into the bloodstream of our universe.

Instinct allows me insight of our healing from the inside out. Therefore discover what we really are on this planet. We require balance of our spheres of mind, body, and soul. We all require balance of our innate energy systems which create integrity of what we are.

No matter the magnitude of imbalance, healing will evolve the remeasurement of all universes, within this universe. The magnitude of our universes is beyond imagination; suffice to say, balance to some extent is constantly in play.

May this drop of sacredness become a piece of the healing which this universe chooses to absorb into its sacredness, so here we can begin to heal together as one hemisphere.

The deepest scars of our collective soul's light illuminates, through its own dance of energies. Throughout its iridescences of consciousness. Its own inexplicableness. Uncloaking darkness to reveal its ignorance, without apologies. Without need of fears or falseness. Without burdens of egotistical justifications or wounding judgements.

This book is my unique mirror interpreting reflections of my true being. It will not call for any mind tools of diminishments. It does not ask of any discriminations or disposals of your individualities. It asks for your integrity with the greatest respect and gratefulness of their hallowed company upon my chosen journeys.

To be reading this at this present moment, no matter your life circumstances at this moment of your journeys, **O**rb has found its way into your hands for a reason today. Your choice of whether you decide to read her, or not, will depend on your individualities. Here and now, I wish to send you my deepest gratitude, along with love, inspiration, and strength of soul, so may you not only live your integrity, but create that endless abundance of sacredness which will construct your spiritual bridge to transverse into our universe of infinities.

If **O**rb has had the honour to have kept you company upon this journey, I too am honoured. I am grateful for your wish to share my company along such a strange and spiritual adventure. An adventure that not only takes one throughout discoveries but creates their own.

If there is a moment in existence, bodies, as well as our souls, allowed to become isolated from our integrity of innocence, creating our essential beings' demise, there our lens of understandings are lost to distortion and the inevitability of loss of our sacredness of spirit.

Incandescence

Let there be light
to see things, you cannot understand
To walk those places too inexplicable
Allow yourself to stand
Within their bright shafts of incandescence
In being more than human will allow
A key is forged in uniqueness
For your hand alone to wield
Then by this power unsheathe your eyes
If you need to be somewhere
Then you must be there
If you are here, reading this
Then you are just where you need to be
If you find what you were looking for
Understand you have much more to learn
This is where hemispheres are aligning
You are only now beginning your journey
Into the shards of your consciousness
And all wondrous realms of your world
While all your life has searched
You find nothing
Here searches your Soul
To discovery
Dare to journey to further Unearth strengths
Both scarred and sacred
This path can all but be reached by warriors
As to return to enlightenment

Where there is no more to seek
No more egos of the mind
But all abundance finds
From the one
light can bring life
There all life can be sustained
As innocence calls you now can listen with voice of one
Who feared to speak but here you shine
Amid the darkest storms to brave this light
Now others may see

Walk with humility
Reach out for the light
Lift your eyes
Reflect your light
Upon those you nurture
Reflections of what you are
Teach strengths
Be the beacon
That can return us home
To all that is innocence
From darkest ignorance
Transformations will aspire
In all our worlds of longings we can become life of a new world
If we dare to dream
Dreams we there evolve
Amid those places
We shall create together

Upon our journeys
To discover consciousness
Into our universe of incandescence
Where nightmares do breathe
Along shadowed corridors of fate
These crawling broken hopes
Which if nurtured
Heal themselves
In such ways
As to strengthen with humilities of wisdom
Far beyond all of man's abandonments
Recall your deepest dreams
There it shall be revealed
Amongst all those times
When all your hopes were lost
You looked much further
Furthest than your strength allowed
But there it was
You found that very thing
A presence you always knew is Here
You allowed your light
There when all your soul
Could see I no longer sought
Hidden no more
We have found of strengths
We found our gate of incandescence

Shards of Innocence

School can contain magic or misery, from a perspective of a child. Realistically both will, for the most contented of children, drag a mixture of these emotional conditions into their world of innocence and drop them onto their clean floors of the daily learning curve. Some will see them as an exciting challenge, others, a messy pile of something they are overwhelmed by, with no idea how to clean it up in the most effective ways.

Their work, their play, what makes them happy in their creative worlds? The very existence of all those elements that build their passions for expressing their individuality, wait in plain sight for just the right times. Time to listen, just listen to that little being on their first unaided strides into their new world of others. As they are given time, attention, empathy, and energy, they will begin to give of themselves in all the best ways imaginable. Agendas of academia can be foundations of creative education. Where co-operation between child and adult creates education that empowers child and educates adult. Reality, sadly, holds a mirror that does not always reflect truth; but something hard to see in the cold light of practicalities.

Understanding can only be effective if both minds learn from each other. Both female and male then are given each other's basic characters in which to learn how they themselves choose their own ways of being. At some point, these different paths will cross. Each will then learn a little bit more about the other's way of being. The eye of this storm, as it were, is silent, is without form, is most powerful when allowed to be absorbed.

Character of the child needs to be held resplendent. That passion they hold is their centre. No matter what the storms bring into their world, their centre of gravity will bind their heart and soul with the substance of warriors. To go beyond sight, sound and thought you, as an adult, are programmed to follow, like an artificial intelligence.

We are all different. Some females are gentle, some confident and outgoing. Some males are gregarious, fearless, some thoughtful, with a will that wishes to protect and nurture, from a compassion that has been before.

This sacredness of child awaits those who wish to see, listen, understand. Somewhere along their path, soon enough as they progress into the next level of schooling, they will take up their character's suit of armour. The toughened layers of being they realise they must, to stand the rigours of life. But for now, first year of schooling has the space for being. Stepping into their own skin. Being allowed space to fly, when and wherever their minds have created most wondrous creations. It does not need to be spectacular, it can be the smallest of ways, but it must not be overlooked, for it is special, it is unique. Allowing time, space, and silence of understanding is where a child can grow in fertile soils of acceptance and remeasurement.

Adults have much to learn from all beings that have just arrived at this realm of existence. The mindset of grownups lends itself to how they can teach anything so new to the planet, all they feel that being needs to learn and therefore understand everything, just so, to arm themselves for future life. Rarely is it the thought that the child enters this world with more wisdom than can be imagined. I believe this to be fact.

Drops in the Ocean

Our greatest gift is our diversity. Yet, for some this engine of creativity is a perpetual cause for contention. Those that nurture a gift as uniquely tuned to nature live lives forged with authenticity. A life so incredibly creative they themselves stand in awe of their own abilities. Wherever and whatever finds the light of their path, sacredness follows.

Within this diversity our ability of communication has capacity to translate all forms of physical, as well as sensory stimuli. If we only but knew, how magical our lives are. Strengths of any species are at their most powerful through their ability to work as one. To achieve this, they evolve a system of simplistic or complex communication techniques. Without such techniques survival would be an extremely terrifying way of existence. In that event of a lone being, having to fend for themselves, life no doubt, is held by a thread far too fragile to sustain healthy existence.

We are drops in the ocean of our galaxy, but these drops contain a magical substance capable of wondrous things. Diversity is a magnetic charge generated from the core of what we are. Diversity is the spark fierce enough to light the torches of ignorance. Diversity will allow light into the darkest chasms of pain and suffering if strength of soul allows. As nature has fashioned her ad infinitum, magnificence is all and more we have been bestowed. To be a species created with differences that complement diversities of nature, is to understand nature's intentions of the effectiveness of those differences.

As a bee colony, nature has evolved this splendid species with differences of similarities. To survive from its innate strengths of diversity, they have evolved specialist adaptations, which allow them to thrive and be their most effective in their specific abilities. Working as one, they are a powerful intelligence. One cannot thrive without the other. Each understanding that through their collectively, they will guarantee optimum quality of life, and through this survive to their optimum potential. The one does not undermine the other. Co-operation and selflessness must be absolute. Yet within this invisibility of oneness, nature ensures nurture of something some humans will not endeavour to concede, integrity of the soul. It needs no materialism, it requires no specialist training, it demands no perpetual praising. It is given. Something sacred emanates from a core of being, an innocence, a knowledge of the importance of our spark of life. Our spark of life understood as beyond our ignorance. They know it. Nature explains this genetic text in many languages within her forms. Some are subtle, some so obvious as to be narcissistic to the extreme, quite bizarre. In nature perceptions are of a higher order. Those of us who know what to look for are fully aware of such a unique code of nature. If you wish to understand, everything is created to nurture everything else.

Identical is something which may be impossible. To be completely identical could be rather a difficult feat to achieve, in any species. Nature is completely unique; therefore, all copies carry their own blueprints. Copies in nature refuse to identify to the letter, even in their own species. The letter here is in constant flux, it, nature, is an extreme gambit of infinite alphabets, both in this world born from the infinity of our galaxies.

Creation will allow freedom of design as much as it can skilfully create. The present moment of its conception calls upon its sacredness to fashion these same molecules with a oneness of the moment that will ensure a difference within its 'prodigy-to-be'. As invisible to the eye, but will be that grain of uniqueness, crafted with magnificence by mother nature herself.

It Is Now

Time has come to meet you
Upon this moment of unrest
You are offered choice
Of how you wish to live your life
Your life that was given
With all sacredness
From all immortalities
Were upon powers of greed
Have no powers
They can only be called upon
From measures of your soul
Upon, and therefore
We must choose now
How we wish to live
Is it not up to us
To choose which stones
Our unique waters flow upon
This river of life's
They though
Need to flow freely
We cannot alter nature
Without Karmic imbalance
We are created with our uniqueness
Of will
In turn to be our nature
We then must nurture its legacy
If ignorance we choose
We alone call upon its consequences
And too shall live their gift

Upon fearful depths of spirit
Be then prepared
To battle all its demons
They will become your friend
As choice was yours
To fill that void of soul
But truth requires
Abundance of all you are
Fearing nothing in This world
Or next
For nothing but soul
Untouchable to all
But sacredness itself
For beings dwells immortal
Within this silent place
It is now
Where all our existence is
It is now
When we have this choice
To learn to Love
In so doing
We learn how to live

Tangerine That Was

Warm in the upper topmost room of the house, a familiar, soft, citrusy aroma caught my senses. My nose knew this pleasant, but perplexing smell, wafting around a specific corner of our spare room. In an instant I realised exactly what it was. Drawn to the hamper on the top of the chest of drawers, I had cleverly compiled for my daughter's working week. They were meant to be picked up with the Christmas presents, sadly they had been overlooked in the excitement, imprisoned by the lack of time. Time though had reminded me in its most graphic way, by disintegrating a piece of fruit. A net of glossy, orange-glow tangerines I had laid on top of the hamper, just because I had them. The honesty of fact is that I love anything tangerine-coloured, tangerines cover every imaginable base in my child-brain. It seemed to fit, Christmas, glittery things, and fruit.

What I had not suspected was the tangerines were anywhere near rotting. Sad, but true, is that one damaged piece will ensure its demise creates a visual masterpiece of luminous green goo, encrusted with a lime green powder puff.

However, stopping to examine the aforementioned fruit, it was obvious to me that this was a case of sacrifice at its highest level. For the other tangerines to stand a chance of survival, this one, the utmost bottom, decided to protect all those in the bag by absorbing the weight stress of each one.

Green, luminescent powder and pulp-gunge was all that was to be seen of what once tangerine was. No sound, no visual movement, not that this event could have been viewed without the aid of a time-lapse camera. And who was to know? Such a covert event as this, would occur so swiftly after the initial deposit. It was all quite unexpected in an unusual sort of way. Therefore, in discovery of the demise of this beloved and bergamot aroma, sphere of neon-citrus, I was devastated.

Soft fruit has a unique life of its own. I am quite sure each fruit has its own decomposition times and sequence of rot. The way of it seems to be that a certain individual will, without delays or distractions, begin its rotting countdown, for reasons only known to it.

Whether the collective has a discussion, or holds a vote is a best kept secret to be sure. But what is for certain, is that there is a containment of the extent of decay, and at any given time, the remaining fruits can be saved from a fate worse than death, waste. Sometimes hidden, sometimes consuming its host in plain sight. My guess? This is surely a choice. Who is to say? Tangerines, as any fruit, may possess their own personalities, good or malevolent. Silently, with stealth, that which looked healthy is suddenly mulched into pulp and pungency, with expert efficiency only nature can replicate. It makes you wonder just how much magic happens every moment of every day.

Another world is right here, under our noses, as it were, doing its thing, living. Nature at work 24/7, in all aspects of life, on all levels, and we just have no idea. How much we miss, is too frightening to contemplate. Would we really be able to comprehend such alchemy? What other layers of life could we then uncover and understand? As much as we believe in our pretext of knowing so much about life and how it works, we are still in the dark about the basic mechanics of what makes life tick. Fruit in all its glory, has its own biodiversity. It has its own universe, which in turn, creates many other universes. From that one seed planted, or the inexplicableness it came into being from, that fruit then has the capability to seed and grow an orchard. The orchard, nurtured to some degree or other, will have the potential to feed endless life forms. Within this process, the lineage of those seeds, in a short span of time, contain the genetic materials to grow thousands of life-enhancing foods. In the space of silence everything speaks to those that wish to listen. The more we attain throughout our lives, the weight of greed becomes heavier. The more we look for our own powers over other weaknesses, we diminish our light upon our life's paths. The more we destroy creation, the love it nurtures, this way of being will manifest itself to seek to consume its source.

Creation is the space, within silence. Creation is all we are and all we require. Creation is the power of all we are, of all we will or shall be. Creation allows that which it has given life to. Every atom of its like. It will not allow that which undoes its nurture. Time and space are the orchards of creation's seeds. From one seed of its creation, life is allowed. This allowance is the seed of sacredness. Creation is the allowance of love. Balance of these elements is essential for nature's flow of life-enhancing energies. Imbalance of energies, destroy creation. To live balanced within this world is to walk with humility. In understanding these things, you understand, you have begun to allow the inexplicableness of creation. It is truly mind-bending.

Belonging Found

That funny day, I opened my back door to greet whoever is
out and about, floating here and there in the hopes of a free
snack. So, there she was, strolling back and forth, not too
obvious, but obvious enough not to be ignored. Violet held
her gaze with an intensity that explained a story. This story
was just for me to read. So, I opened her spell-binding book
and became enthralled. She walked along my back garden
wall, with a slight hunch that showed me she was fearful and
timid of almost anything. As I looked at her, she watched me
with a wise intensity I knew all too well. In a swift moment
she carefully made her way down the stone steps and there,
in a jiffy she was in. She chose to sit, quite still on my kitchen
floor and look at me with her marble-green eyes. A gaze able
to speak, without any need of words. But as I looked back, I
could see that her eyes were not just any old green, oh no!
These were a green I had rarely come across, flecked and
speckled with copper, that caught light to beam it back, as if
plugged into an electric socket. They took me back to my jar
of rainbow-coloured glass marbles. They glowed, as if
illuminated from inside. You know that glitter nail varnish,
where the glitter suspends itself within the colour? Her eyes
were glitter orbs, bronze glitter suspended within a rich,
earthy jade colour. Never had I seen such eyes outside a
documentary on wild cats.

The more I looked, the more of a strange, unsettling
feeling I had. It was not that they were scary, but that they
seemed to see into my very soul.

So, there we were, staring at each other for what seemed a

lifetime. In fact, it was only around three minutes. I then heard myself asking, 'Fancy a bite to eat little girl?'

From that moment life has never been the same. Violet has been absorbed into our family. She would not have it any other way. Never could anything, or anyone surpass the amount of food eaten in any one sitting. Little did I know, this odd-shaped little furry-bod could consume three ton of chicken, fish, canned foods, and the occasional dip into a dish of sardines or like-minded assortments. But you know what? It is all right. As I was to discover, this little furry bod would teach me many wondrous things, never imagined in a million years, or more.

Soon after that meeting, Violet moved in. As if she had never lived anywhere else. If asked, she no doubt would explain this sentiment too. Using the litter tray had obviously been omitted from her daily regime. A particular patch of my living room carpet lay testament to this fact. Just when I had depressingly resigned myself to living within a festering bog of eternal stench, Violet evolved into a highly efficient toileting machine. Her co-ordinates and soil-tray mapping were second to none. This was the miracle I needed in my hectic, illogical, highly nurtured, insane and spontaneous life. We now have a viable bond, highlighted by regular mind-melding moments, which to the normal eye will appear quite scary.

Work nights are pre-programmed with an exacting, yet exhausting routine. From a certain hour the crew (all four felines) are fed supper in two parts. I scuttle about like a community of along a garden path woodlice in the moonlight, with an exacting agenda of de-barking a small tree, just before break of dawn. As for our new family member, she has mastered the psychic art of positioning herself exactly at the correct angle of optimal vision. Once hypnotised, I am then programmed to go directly to her feeding platform, tucked into the corner of our kitchen. If I have the audacity to take too long dishing out the mixed grill of the evening, she squeaks her comical, soprano squawk, giving me the evil eye, unapologetically. By this time, I am pretty convinced I have grown at least two more sets of limbs, none of which are working to my benefit. Once the motley-crew are with their meals, then, if I have not had the intelligence to have prepared myself for work, inevitably the dark mist descends upon the last vestige of sanity I possess. Mentally clawing at any crumbs of logic I may possess.

Approaching home somewhere after 7am, as if by magic two of my incredible little crew appear. Then the third, then, a form of darkest, blackest velvet slides out into the soft light of the porch. A source of sound I know extremely well pierces the dawn silence, Violet. Key finding its lock, all of pandemonium is unleashed. As we all tumble out and into the porch, our agenda is as clear as mud. So, where has my magic wand disappeared today? Then, as I stop in mid-flight, lost in the confusion, Violet sits, looks into my soul, and we both smile.

Infinitum

To be an infinite drop of sacredness
Poured into fire and fierceness of unkind elements
We must find our way through
This alchemy of existence
And all we are within it
And we have a place here
An important a place
That we are still unsure
With every waking day
There is a mission to partake
If we cannot see
We must look to the skies
And move moon itself
To tilt upon our path
So as to light our way.
Then be not afraid of fearful things
Which wish to wound our souls
For when all is told
We are earth's warriors
To stand amid such storms
That would tear your heart into a thousand pieces
This is our journey throughout bitter winds
Unrelenting upon our purest consciousness
Times visit where we are left alone
Amid unspeakable demons
Dare walk this earth
Yet if we stand our ground
All will find its place

To converge as something beautiful
As innocence born to nurture
Candescent as the bridge of rainbows
Flowing back into the rivers of our dreams
Such dreams that will make love grow miraculous
All life incredible
Let us be there to be unyielding.
To all but the sacredness of this life
If such tasks are far too fearful
Then call my name
For I am here
Without need for falseness
Masks of miseries and maladies of heart
All is possible within
To live as one great tree
Our roots need to grow connected
We need nurturing from this sacred earth
We need its sustenance
We need as our breath of life

Growing Flowers

Loving you grows me like a flower
You love me so much it makes me grow
To have a mum
Or to have a dad
One may do the job of two
Sometimes it can be so very tough
Raising a child or children
Even so,
If you give all you are
More on difficult days
You will be loved endlessly
I know what is good
Because there you are
Doing your best as always
Here you are my loving parent
Always holding out your arms
Waiting for me to run towards you
I know where I will be unharmed
I know just where to find you
Because you are always here in my heart
No one else but you
This perfect feeling in my soul
Are your nurturements in my heart
They look after me when I slip out of my bed
With sleep still in my eyes
You carry with your strength
Here I can walk with confidence
You talk with me from your wisdom
I can understand what I need to be

You nurture me with your perfect love
I will find my own will
To be that better person
When all others are unwilling
To be all that they can be
You have brought me into this world
I am so grateful for all you have given
My heart and soul are your design
Forever I shall wear your love
Forever your love shall be mine
With every breath and every wish
Nevermore to want more
I have more than wealth I have all
More than wished for
This sacredness of being nurtured
By a mother
By a father
It matters to be loved
By someone who really loves you
Is to be blessed by angels themselves
I so do understand
That you are my guardian angel And I belong with you

Language of Universe

Communication is a most powerful means to any given
situation
Poverty has a lack of connectiveness
Where we will not prosper as one race
We lose our wealth of sharing
Our innateness of the powers of sharing
Carries with it this momentum
That can open locked doors
Offerings of achieving miraculous outcomes
You never thought possible
Breaking through chains of exclusions
Bolted down with confusions
That corrode your very soul
Communications keep you whole
Like spheres in our universe
They give you pause for thought
Dismantle mental structures
Explain facts of impossibilities
Illuminate all hidden possibilities
You can never know all there is in this world
It is not for us to uncover the future
Only remnants and regrets of our past
There is a place where all will be revealed
But not here and now
You may think life owes you everything you wish
Do not fool yourself it is just another chore
You really do not need
To hide behind a mask

But some that have everything
Locked into a dark room
With no handle on their door
Part of us knows
The mind will only tolerate so much pretence
It then begins to create a way to build a fence
And all those hiding behind
Still will not understand why they are there
They cannot see this green space
For the mask upon an empty face
Lost in ignorance
Then how to find the seeds
Set root in our minds of fertile places
But it is rotated all right side up
When they look in the mirrors of deception
Just be sure not to mention
What you really see on the dark side of your mind
Because you never know what you will find
In the wee small hours of your dreams
They are not always as they seem
And it happens all too much
By the process of miscommunication
Our default system of psychological games
Cry into your wealth
If you feel you must
It is only your word
Against those you do not trust
What an ingenious master plan
So intricate
It would fit inside a sardine can
But I am not a fan

Truth is all about what is real

In this universe where life is born
Forever waiting for the moment of our dawning
Into consciousness
In this miraculous social condition
That requires no wealth
Just a willingness to grow together
Brave this storm of fearful mind-weathers
And just communicate as one
Where you are given more than you could ever need
Sharing just the smallest of moments
For what we need is a splash in our oceans
Nothing more would be undone
And the Allness of all our beings
That share this immense event called life
Brought here to enhance the infinite powers
Of our imaginations
We have no comprehension of how we came to be
So many plausible theories
Give it that sound of surety
But we have the skills to create marvellous designs
Of our infinite minds
We have no idea of the inexplicableness we can find
It is too long a time
Where we still have not learned
How to live in this place
This magical space
Where we can grow and evolve
Into something incredible

Past is our journey of discoveries

It gives us answers to questions we would rather not ask
We can rummage through our discarded nightmares
We would rather not share with the child in us
But as a child
Did we not ask too many questions?
We grow strong
Understanding all that we should
To give of ourselves for the betterment of all
When we have not grown half as much
As we often think
When truth be told
We possess wealth
Poverty remains in materialistic manipulation
Something too fearful amidst poorest populations
You live happy with
Or die pitifully without
But some cannot see beyond the wall
Only one thing to do
When you take a fall
Look up and pull yourself up
If there is no one left around
I can always find a circle of beautiful friends
Who I call 'the engineers'
They can build
They can create
They are cause to be thankful
For this state of existence called life
What has it all been for?
How did we keep ourselves on the other side of
That locked door of communications?

> I have become warrior
> All and more I bear the scars

Of whom and what I am
All this beauty our earth emanates
Wondrous creations beyond compare
The infinitesimal moments to nurture
A world without ignorance
Knowledge from destructive past hates
Replace exclusion with Inclusions
Nurture without abandonments
Rebuilding present neglects
In constructing this world of humanities
Enlightenment by all working together
The unceasing will to create good
To become all and then more
For without this our invitation to life
Will become our paradise no more
We need to learn
What it has all been for?
Centuries of evolvement
Learning and understanding why we are here
Now there is no time left
We are being asked to give
Our existence requires we share
There is a universal law
That governs us
So that we may keep balance
To give love
To grow within its light
For all and each being
In so doing
We then become strength itself

To complete this sphere of nations
Within earth's healing of our communication

Communication is our means to an end
Of poverty
Communities broken from our oneness
Global destruction
Replaced by structures our ego's
Imbalance of wealth
Suffocation by stealth of power
Ignorance of intelligence
Absorbed into our psyches
There to teach us selfishness
Time has arrived to live consciously
Where those who have nothing
But must work to give all
Can find their dignity
Work with gratitude
Choice is always a given
But do we have such luxuries?
This is not a dream
It is a reality
Of that which nightmares are made of
Where humanity has chosen ways
To close a sacred door on its innate possibilities
Communication is a means to an abundance of
individualities
Everything that has abilities
To create our freedoms
It speaks all languages
It can forge the keys of the heart
To unlocking universal doors of ignorance

It is the chance to learn
It is the teacher of understandings

It is the multitude of warriors
That will rescue and protect the child
Who will
In turn light our way out
From this tomb of dark destruction
Losing your will to be free
From the tides of ego's powerful seas
Washing over your true self
There goes your wealth of self-respect
Like a virus that wants to infect
But you cannot find an antidote
So, you leave a note
And I quote
'If in the event of you finding these words
I hoped someone would have communicated before time ran
out'
And I called out so many times
But nobody cared'
Now it is up to those of us
That wish to learn
Just how to live together

Returning Together

In softest moonlight you sleep
And all our stars are watching over
Innocence embraces your heart
Where all our dreams are restored anew
The smallest drop of goodness will work its magic
Within an ocean of suffering
This space between that and these
Chant gently through the night
If you will not understand something clearly
There is always a friend waiting
You will see through your darkness
Life still goes on like a marching band
It pours through the creases and cracks in our hands
Without noticing it is almost tomorrow
Then time will catch us while we are unaware
Whether you create a good place
To find that part of your heart that is lost
It will find you
Or whether you cannot find yourself at all
The smallest drop of goodness will work its magic
Within an ocean of silent sufferings
This space between this and that
Makes strange sounds throughout the night
Learn now to understand something clearly at last
And can teach others to see beyond their darkness
As our life still goes on like a marching band

But we can grow with it here
We offer more than our taking ever can
Yes, now it is tomorrow
Always catching us unawares
We have nurtured such a good place
All mended that which was lost
Here we are as this oneness
And together we can find our way together

Beyond Light

At some point in our lives
We have a choice of direction
Along those paths
We can choose to see
To see beyond darkest shadows
We can choose where this terminator lies
And in this choosing
We alone have more than powers
But create our sacred dreams
So there awake to summon
All our soul into this night

Where life has broken us
We must heal our wounds
To understand these scars
We dare not hide them
As beauty holds the truth
We must stand amid illuminations
To see ourselves in our own light
All the impossibilities we are
Moreover, we are more than senses do allow
We of beings magnificent may choose
More than we must dare allow
We together
Hold this key
Turn its lock
Allow our universe
To 'let there be light'

(Genesis. 1:3).

Are We Just a Dream?

I am rock of immovability
I protect all that is
All who wish to find refuge
Within my weathered being
I am a place of peace
Where nothing can harm you
I am this light
From Which all can see
All that you wish to be
I am windows into
Those darkest rooms
Of all you fashion
Allowing light to heal what is
Whoever sees through
Will discover how to live
A way to live free
I am fire consuming
Falseness and destructive fear
I cleanse your soul
With air to allow nurturements
I keep its flame
Through darkest night
I shall be here
Within change I shall remain
I am day
That frees the sun
I hold this light
Where shadows cast their marionettes
Upon the tapestry of your soul

Dancing as sunbeams
Upon silence of a gentle day
I am that place
Where moon and sky
Paint magic upon our stars.
Inside the minds of dreamers
Here our stars lie dusted upon midnight skies
As past midnight slips into my dreams
I see eagles of a thousand worlds
They call to me
Show me which way to go
As all the while
I feel that I have wings
When all the while
I speak with words I do not know
All the while the sky
Melts inside my room
Through frosted glass that glistens
With diamonds fashioned
From ice and moonlight
It seems that all the world has paused
I gaze to find the moon
And there you are
Resting contently upon my eyes

We can but see
We can but know
Those things that only we wish to dream
Hold out your hands
You can touch the sky
Wrap yourself in a passing moonbeam
This is where you dream
But you have awoke

In time for the passing storm
That has now fallen into earth.
And in this maze of lost intentions
I see you there
I see you waitin
Time calls to those who care to listen
Asking where we go from here?
But how can you know the way home
When you know not
Where you have been?
There you were already
It could be that
It is time to learn
How to create a home
Where we can all live
Within your mind's eye
And journey back
This home of earth

Find me I am warrior
Learn to listen to our guardian angels
They have come to show us how to reach their light
While night awaits
Our restless dreams
Its dawn reclaims their silence
Are we merely just a dream?

Biscuit In My Airing Cupboard

I opened the cupboard and there it was. Truth is you discover more than you ever thought possible when you lose something, anything.

We all believe we are so hard done by whenever we lose something of worth to us. It could be something unimpressive, could be an item of great sentimental, emotional wealth, in the world of human values.

Although there is something in this world, something that many humans do not value whether because they cannot see it, do not wish to, or cannot find the capacity to understand it, is the capacity to value the infinitesimal universes of life within our world.

The element I refer to is Love. A small word I agree, but this word contains all the contents of the universe and no doubt, far, far, beyond.

As one day happened, as they do, I fell across a spider in my back garden. Yes, I said fell, as that is exactly what I did. In my haste to get the top of the garden I tripped over my own toe; it is the one I can always rely on to trip me up when in a rush or being casual as occasionally happens. I can always rely on my second toe, the one next in line to my big toe on my left foot, to work its magic.

As if it has been assigned to do so, tripping me up is what it can do in the most elegant of ways. I find myself switching on my cautious walk. It is a slower, more deliberate mode of striding towards any given object, or terrain. Quite often, more than I would like. Certain footwear can summon my altered state of gait. This must be a known quirk of one's person that others must suffer from, or is it a personal idiosyncrasy of my specific toe configuration?

So, this stranger than usual day, my big feet, or foot, had arranged an excursion in my little time bubble for the day. Reconfiguring my limbs amidst my disgruntlement and disappointment at my habitual clumsiness, I heaved myself up as elegantly as a bull elephant and smiled as if I was the wisest creature that had lips. I have no idea why I smiled, but it felt so good. It could be the realisation that things could have been so much worse, and I could have found myself bonded, at a molecular level to our moss-covered wall, a rustic monolith that had grown an emerald green and was now a magnificent metropolis for every bug created upon this planet.

Lifting my head to refocus my bearings as which way was uppish, there, held in mid-doings was a large and well-appointed spider. Her body was so healthy that it glistened and shimmered in the warmth of our peaceful afternoon together. While my brain was switched off, there was nothing else for it but to sit down on my pondering and just be.

Unbeknown to the degree of normality I possessed here was a perfect moment. This moment held everything of everything within its unsuspecting, droplet of time. So, something held me in its grip. Suspended in the beautiful web of this awesome arachnid, my mind swaying on her line of strongest gossamer thread. I had decided there was something about the way she held herself, lithe, elegant, an exquisite huntress. We kept company for what was an unmeasurable time, we had no plans as it happened. Our huge ball of Saturday's sunshine was sinking into the promise of its dusky cloak. Nothing would ever touch such a moment in the same way again, we both understood.

There it was, the call of normality. Half an hour before suppertime was due to be reckoned with, immediately that sharp feeling of accountability began to claw its way out of my head. The memories were lucid, tangible to the senses. I felt the inner workings of mind, body and spirit gather them all up and selfishly store them away in an untouchable cupboard in amongst my uplifting spiritual universe, sacred, held in highest regard, immortal. Once returned to the kitchen, a minor readjustment of my visual cortex, I scanned the inner recesses of the food shelves and adeptly slid out my selection of ingredients, smug in my self-culinary expertise, I would transform any boring feeding feast into a rather mouth-watering evening meal with good company thrown in for free. I have regarded this as a super-positive trait.

You cannot beat a little self-praise I say.

With new perspective, and in sight of my newly awakened contentiousness, I gently made my way back to beautiful Jewel, this would be spider's name. She was no longer swaying from her flower stalk, but had floated across the soft, spongy moss across her gossamer tightrope, into the cool, shaded pocket of her fragrant corner adorned with stalagmites of thick, soft forget-me-nots which looked like miniature, purple Christmas trees. Suspended above hung the silver network of an elaborate web, speckled with unfortunates that had strayed too close.

This latest stash of unfortunates was wrapped in her silver twine. We were both in synch with each other and made busy for nurturing ourselves for the evening and night's rest, as well as creativities to come. We are, after all, quite unique little beings, not given to normality to any degree.

Finding You

Being is something that transforms whatever it touches. You become it. It needs company. This is a new day, how about taking it for a walk.

If you have a best friend that you can make time for. To be a good friend is one of the loveliest things in this whole, busy-bee world. Whenever you feel that this world is too busy for you that day, just sit in a quiet place. Become quiet. Think things that you wish to keep you company for that moment. Happy things. Those things that are your best friends whenever you need them. They might have always been there. When you were a little child, they found you one day, or night, and stayed with you because you both knew nothing would ever keep you apart in the whole of your busiest, busy-bee life.

And if it's fair to say, your whole world has been transformed by, and in this universe of inexplicableness. To believe in something, anything that is not visible, is to ask too much of almost anyone. Who in their right mind would believe in such things. Surely belief is as a certainty. A knowing of whatever has questioned your sanity is, for the better part, held in truth. Though you see, life will not give this certainty of credentials. It is up to us to prise apart the outer shell of uncertainties, teeth and all, delve in and pick up, examine, analyse and choose our diagnosis. Living within the orb of being is becoming your true self. Your integrity engages to its full potential.

There is a peace unlike any other. The pages of days are turned by you. They have their own story. Their words are your deeds. Thought walks beneath a different light. Where life was as a distant place which required your compass to navigate the prevailing weathers of passing circumstances, not an easy feat for the most unflinching of navigators.

Within being no external equipment is required. You are its captain, you its passenger, weather bears no power in this dimension of the soul. You are the eye of the storms of experience, and so all that is lives within your experiences. It breathes through you. It is nurtured by you. It shall evolve from you. There is no beginning of this phenomenon of consciousness. It has always been. Empires risen, fallen men of powers and pride have faded like ink upon ancient parchments. But for that time greatness flew as a phoenix, only to become the flames that would light the endless torches that lined those crumbling corridors of our past.

What of our past? That spectre of mind that lies silent inside jagged, abstract thoughts. Silence that screams at the broken windows of our perceptions. Echoes of its spirit haunt the abandoned castles of contentments and leave their fears to seed the cracks of our endless insecurities. In the here, within this breath of possibilities is a resurrection of our purpose, our perception. There is a palpable heartbeat. Education, for me, is derived from knowledge of our past, but not its acceptance of its lessons. I am perplexed by history. For all its factuality of evidence, impact leaves me mortally wounded. As default my want is to learn lessons from the past. I rescue, transport to my place of safety, with another guidance tool wisely chosen to add to my psychic wizardry, to be accessed upon a moment's notice, to be examined, to be investigated beneath an alternate light. Those specialist skills required are then taken into care by my higher mind, my alternate existences, my true self.

If, and only if, I am able to save any viable life from this entity of past, I will do everything in my newly identified powers to resurrect it. That which remains, I intend to nurture with all the intensity of the warrior I am.

Dreams long held by the ether of our strengths. Dreams we dare dream, because they are that voice left amid the darkness of this earth's despair. To dream as a child is to nurture that which is innocence, that which returns us, I feel. All we are dwells without need of our external tending or attention on any level of our existence.

Working with anything or anyone who lives without the affliction of ego is where I live with knowledge of a oneness of my spirit. There is no substitute, it is alignment of my spirit with my soul. From this pendulum of possibilities time is held suspended, to await all that I am. In the light of something or someone that is all that they dream, is to live this dream of life. Starfish dreamt they could one day become stars, if they dreamt with all their hearts. When you wish with your mind, you dream with your being. Community kept them strong and compassionate; they all helped each other with whatever was needed to be done. Nothing was too much of a trouble; in the doing of this they learnt how being together as one entity nurtured them in a wondrous way. You see, starfish see life as a fabulous adventure. The journey is a part of this adventure, but it is the working together which creates magical things.

Magic has the potential to create the most inexplicable events known to humankind. Some things move in the strangest ways, whether you want them to or not.

As they swam for such a long, long, time in the deepest seas, they never stopped dreaming.

Night after night they looked up at the skies and wished. Everything they did throughout each busy day held the silent words, words they did not need to speak as they all knew exactly what these words were and what they meant. They all possessed highly evolved instincts. Instincts they had learnt to use as their own symbiotic language so long ago that even they had forgotten how long ago it was.

Stars shimmered back at the communities of starfish. They too had their own special language, a universal language It is the way of things, how communication happens. Sound is physical. Instinct something ethereal. Ethereal is that silent feeling you feel when no one else needs to speak or fills your mind with things they want to be filled with.

In my world, to cross these two worlds is to cross a bridge that cannot be seen, cannot be heard, cannot be touched, cannot be taken away. This language is not an earthly language. It can only be spoken within our being. It lives within our souls. Its powers can only come into being through the alchemy of nurture. Nurture is the food on which instinct grows. Nurture is the food on which instinct thrives. Nurture is the food on which instinct creates its bridge. This instinct can only then travel across this bridge to the source of your being, your soul, to speak through your heart, arriving at its destinations that lie within the intrinsic of your essential being. As previously stated, this is most definitely my world.

Our Kitchen of Contentments

Key in the door, it has been a long day today. Turning to look at our row of loved-in-lived-within chunky, chocolate-tinted houses. They smile back at me, winking their softly glowing windows. It is a little after late from work, and my tummy complains 'hurry in! I'm starving!'

Where the cold hits the heat of our luminescent lobby, goosebumps paint my skin in a fine layer of chill. I am speckled with evening's spring reminder, mother nature's motherly advice. I need to keep my favourite woollies in fluffy rotation next to my backpack. Some things in a working girl's life are essentials, some things you think about far too much, then make the wrong decision. Deep down there is a perpetual battle with logic and limitations of intelligence. I believe it is a war already won and not necessarily by every individual within our species, certainly not me.

In the face of adversity humans have immense capacity to achieve impossibilities. This being so, how then are we lost in these same abilities, by destructive elements, that if left to their own devices can undo any number of hard-fought achievements? Strength of soul comes from overcoming forces much stronger than human makeup can comfortably endure. It is within, and must then become, an inexplicableness that you alone must forge. An out-of-body alchemy you alone possess in its uniqueness of chemistry. A one-off amalgamation of emotional damage, depth of compassion, integrity of spirit and wisdom of warriors. In reaching this order, you carry a strength no one, or nothing can dismantle.

Arrival into the kitchen via the stairs of a thousand sleepy steps, held out its arms for me to snuggle inside its spicy-warmth and cushioned couches. To be home is to find all those places in your dreams you go to whenever your mind is screaming for comfort. Whenever you are needing solitude kitchen is where this lives and breathes, like an entity that knows where you are, what you are thinking, always ready there with hot cuppas, scrumptious foods and copious, colourful, quick-drying nurturing for the soul, our souls.

It is where your faith in human nature can be restored or recalled. Whatever the time, kitchen will research and rebuild a broken heart, a wounded spirit, inspire your deranged thinking to return to its logical and rightful place in your psyche, teach you the importance of being silly, just as a matter of course. Happiness fills a homely kitchen to where you feel it immersing you, like sliding into a warm frothy bath on a bitingly, chilly day. Warm chocolate couches wait to melt you into their soft, shiny leather, immediately asking 'go on then, tell me about your day'?

Weekends will give you options of being sociable, talk about this and that, wear funny hats while comparing who has the most bizarre socks inside slippers, that have grown around every curve of your feet, floppy and fluffy, fraying where the soles meet. Kitchen is our place we meet and greet, without malice or ill intent, it finds our best sides, then freeze-frames, rewinds and teaches us how to learn. In the chit and chat that hovers in thick, bright clouds and nestles in sticky clumps just under the pastel-coloured shelves that suspend our emporium of sugared scrummiest dried fruits sleeping within spices, all sorts of niceties too good to try to describe. These are things only spoken of once eaten, in special moments requiring serious snacks. Time cannot be altered, but it can be relaxed. When it comes to clocking off the rat race for the day, our clock 'bedtime!' Ha! There is always time though, for that top-up to finish our conversation. You know, this kitchen is where we unravel these problems of our world, speaking so much sense that we laugh at our wisdom, in our realisation of how important we are in this world, but also understanding our scattiness and insanities are much needed by our own sanities.

Because our thoughts and wishes are filled with so much integrity from the heart, I know that the magic of our love in our kitchen squeezes through the keyholes and fills up the skies with nurture. Because of love, the integrity of love, the unyielding properties of love, life around it wishes to be there. It wishes to live and breathe all things invisible floating within its ether. You can feel it. It clings to your soul, without you asking. You knowing you are even more incredible for it. Love propels itself along the colours of energies we create within our chakras. There is a conversation of compassion in constant communication, allowing each sense a safe place to dwell at any given time. A dance of incomprehensibilities, in celebration of our sacredness. Our very existence is intertwined with our universe at an atomic level. We are everything we wish to be at any given time. Space and time are one as we ebb and flow throughout its magnificence, that is our sea of existence.

As I dissolve into the sanctuary of my late-evening kitchen's silence and the sounds of its resting breath from our hectic cafe hours, I close my eyes in front of our glowing fire, just sighing its last murmurings for today.

My toes are so warm and toasty, wiggling off miseries of gripes and growls' hectic days. Here, in the hug of my hands is the purple-polka-dot mug that always comes to my aid in any psychic emergency. Filled with the dark frothiness of chocolate, submerged beneath those jewelled colours of squishy marshmallows that defy gravity and demand your biggest grin. But you know! There is no such phenomenon as time in our kitchen. When we three females are all in place, like the meeting of the high council of Jedis, nothing is impossible to undo any destructive force. We have most graciously evolved the art of reconstructing any sort of collateral life damage known to our species. Once the topic is brought to our fabulously, food-laden table, we arrange ourselves into our special thrones of authority. Whoever needs a particular problem dismantling, they take centre stage to position their spotlight. There they can highlight their gripe or confusions, ideas or fears upon the matter concerned.

No restraints or judgements are allowed. Nothing but compassion, understanding and an active participation in empathy. Whatever the day, or night's debate agenda, the goal is to achieve and maintain peace and integrity in our universe of us. Our cats, as is always the case, are chief overseers of the forum, they are law. So, when our conclusion hour arrives, they alone psychically link in to pass their wisdom. It is all this simple, yet the mechanics of our 'serious seminars' are extremely important to the insane workings of our household. Here is where our laws and veggie lasagne begin.

Back gardens, we have discovered, are biospheres of another kind. Close encounters with our back garden ensure we, collectively, keep our busy feet firmly anchored to mother earth. There is a corner we have created for the sole purpose of meeting at some point in any day.

Rain or sunshine, we attract each other's attention to the need for sustenance of some form. A teapot stands testament to our love of all things cuppa. It stands as a sentinel all through the week, under our large tepee that we three created from a bunch of tarpaulins we found in a bargain sale corner of one of our favourite bargain stores. The ropes and ties we also found there, so that day was an epic cake and cuppa moment, with us all inflicted with that painful condition where you cannot stop laughing. Next day was not so funny, though, as we realised how complex this was going to be. It took us a whole weekend to find the best way of constructing it, but we did learn the perplexing sextet to happiness as a result. I had no belief in my construction abilities until that weekend. Also, my fragile skills of spontaneous design were most certainly put to the test. By the Sunday lunchtime this pyramid of plastic prisms had bonded us indelibly together. It was as if we could create anything we wished in our own magical world of nurturement and knowing. It is us to a tee! Whether snow, wind, or summer's sweat, our tepee keeps us grounded in our little orb of extraordinariness. The garden itself has grown into its own space of individualities, as we call it. Wild bits here and there. If the weeds do not pose a threat to wildlife and limb, we make sure they are happy here. Buckets of odd shapes, dings, holes, bent and buckled, all belong with us. Wildlife has need of any old containers that can home them, in all their shapes and sizes, it is just how things are meant, and we are here to make certain that is just how it is. Life in its essence comes to our gardens, maybe for a visit, maybe for a long vacation, maybe for life, we have no clue, and we really do not give a snapdragon! Our mission is to be here, there, or wherever our situation desires, come hell or hiccups, and we have no control over the amount of goodness that emanates from us. The more the better that we can eliminate through our insanities of illuminations. First thing as I can get myself outside is to go and top up any containers, likely feeding receptacles, happy corners of nature's eco-friendly cafés for our eclectic mix of beloved communities, be it those passing through or permanent residents. If the time happens that I have no time, I make sure I choose the most important choice, so I go feeding my clan of a billion little souls no matter who, what, and why. You see it is about what kind of universe you wish to create. That soulless place where life, any life, has no meaning to you, or that place in your soul where nothing else is allowed, only love. As a family, we three females have chosen. In this overwhelming, fast-flowing, self-serving materialistic world, we decided to live in our sacredness. Not too shabby a shack, in the light of the alternatives.

This inexplicable gentility, patient selflessness earned through the art of understandings and nurturements. We allowed ourselves to become who we are meant to be. It asked nothing from us. It just keeps giving.

Universe of Sock

Two of something that works as a nurturing force, always
feels right. In particular, that mysterious subject of socks.
Emotions can run into exhausting moments, sometimes in
ways you never thought possible, after all socks are socks.
That drawer designated to the world of undies I have found
to contain a rather secret life of its own, both hostile and
friendly. Some of those items where time has wreaked havoc,
find themselves shadowy corners thriving for untold numbers
of years. No amount of logic, home husbandry, constructive
energies or a powerful will-to-live counter-checks their
abilities of mutation. Two, become that furiously frustrating
sinking feeling, magnetised to those bits of you, you rather
held their integrity, in the hope of fooling yourself that you
are a highly efficient human.

Fabric frayed, faded colours, frazzled elastic constructs too
tired to give any more of their life-support, as they require
more of it themselves. Things resembling stuff you bought
some time ago, far too long ago as it turns out. Screams
reminding you to go and shop for replacements, yet there
they are, grinning it seems for the next millennia, defying
you to sort through their tonnage of tat holding you to
ransom, plain mean. In that occasional mind-storm when
you have gained enough strength to actually pull out a
gnarled remnant or two, there is a silence, an awareness of
hope. In that brave moment, taken an eternity to arrive at,
there is a wave of elation so strong you can see yourself do
and become anything you ever wished to become. You feel
invisible. All this stems from a fraught and fiendish history of
one-sock syndrome. Once lived this tumultuous way of life,

my belief is that you never do escape the order of the sock. Believe me I have tried, experienced the pure happiness of spring-cleaning environmental control, but to no avail. During a matter of days, maybe hours, they have found me. Human possibilities aside, it is not humanly possible. If NASA have sock drawers in their pristine white gloss, state of the arts facilities, I know they too are in the order. It is not something wealth nor intelligence is able to infiltrate, it is as a karmic law. Not something spoken about in everyday life, a secret society known to be out there, but far too intimidating to chit-chat about to just anyone.

Don't get me wrong, societies are my kind of thing in nurturing, healthy contexts. However, something with the power to play your sense of realities on a daily basis constitutes a mind control only found in the pages of George Orwell's spine-chilling novels. When you understand the mechanics of such an alternate universe, life can never be the same again.

My out and about socks are, in essence, mismatched. If they are without significant holes, they work for me. On the other foot, holes I grade by size and positioning. If that hole is of no great size, I overlook it as being a character trait. Positioning, it must be said, is rather complex. Toe holes are non-acceptable for journeys of a social nature, town, friends' visits, important errands. Quality of sock is an essential ingredient when it comes to non-work endeavours. Working out hole position, along with quality of sock takes a skill few may possess. Though this sounds implausible I gain a strange satisfaction from my abilities of sock assignment. Colours are where I excel, without a doubt.

My pallet heavily leans to summer and autumn, occasionally it has been known that I snatch a brace of a colour that surprises me. Through years of sock selection, my choice of materials is no less that exocentric. It would make my life to discover corduroy, lined with teddy-fleece. Thinking of it, you could possibly find slippers with this make-up, but I mean lightweight socks. Unless it is the height of summer, I am a freezer, so this combination of oddity would fit my mental remit for one happy customer. When working out the wheat from the chaff in our psychological clutter, some things matter a whole lot more than some other things. I find feeling cosy, with a heart filled with happy, is not only the foundation of what makes me tick but is an intrinsic ingredient in what makes my ticking so distinctive. Little stuff nurtures me in my essence. It pours into my thoughts without being asked. Things overlooked by the hub and bub of our must do's. Things drizzled around the pillars of our rolling agendas. Madness conjured up by perpetual needs, wants, greeds and self-fulfilling existence. Small stuff brings you down to this solidity, this natural pungency, this balance emanating from fine cracks throughout the faulty, emotional architecture supporting overwhelming forces of human nature. Heaven knows any fates of the human condition, as only it could. Conditions may be treatable; they may become something that defies intervention. When you take things apart in your mind, wracked with that haunting book of questions, without answers, socks, you will undoubtedly find, will take backstage. Because socks are a colourful, secret universe unto themselves.

The more you try to understand, the less you know which end is up. It is a paradox of life, especially ours.

Pieces of Time

Pieces of time peel away in the passing of circumstance
Flaking into the earth's mantle
With forgotten hopes
Wrapped inside abandoned dreams
They call like children lost

All is not lost here in this world we need to understand
There is much to learn now
Being is working as one
In this day we must nurture
In this day we must grow

Pieces of time peel away in our passing of knowledge
Waiting for our love and devotion
Given without need
While we allow all we are
For the good of all
All given for the good
This good we can give
To grow all that is good

When we look back in time
Be sure to open both eyes
See all there that awaits
Waiting for you here
Allow it to be incredible
At the crossings of time and space
We need to choose which way we face
Whether storm or a paradise of graces
Hates are destructions

Parasites or demons wearing human faces
To take courage upon your shoulder
There to find where hells do hide
See all from the light within
Your eyes shall throw its light
Maybe your toils will be too heavy
But your soul will lift upon angel's wings
Believe your soul's purpose
It is your mirror
It is where light enters
There you will discover
This sacredness that will carry you home

As I Am

With the breath that I breathe
I shall be all that I can be
With the beat of my heart
I shall allow my universe
To grow strong
To live within its integrity
With each move that I take
I shall be all that I can be
With each beat of my heart I shall give
With this sound that I hear
I shall be all that I can be
With the beat of my heart I shall understand
I shall be all that I can be
With this sight into light
I shall learn
I shall be all that I can be
With consciousness of thought
With these deeds I endeavour
I shall be all that I can be
With forethought of being
I shall be
With my uniqueness of life
I shall be all that I can be
With knowledge of sight
I shall be
With this choosing of paths
I shall be all that I can be
With allowing this nature
I shall be

With all I can be
I shall be all that I can
With sacredness that I am
I shall be all
Where we are
Shall be sacred
All we are
Shall be sacredness

Power of Self

Finding your way through life is a perilous journey at the best of times. To be rich, or to exist unto that life where living is mostly happy, and any daily obstacles can be overcome with minimal effort. Within the remaining percentage of human existence, the precarious mechanics of invisible interactions will unquestionably create diverse designs within our infinitesimal universal psyche. But you know, it is not all gloom upon doom, having less of things can become more without you understanding anything about such a questionable state of existence.

Amid not having, not owning, not given access to, there is a place where you alone can access. Within this lesser reality there is an inexplicable abundance. Though your mind will cling to its base emotions for the grimmest of lives, you do not have to adhere to its demands, there is another inexplicable world you do possess, that no one, or no circumstances can take from you. This world I am referring to is a realm of your being always accessible, as mentioned before, always waiting for you to engage with its protective gate, one which only you have been blessed with its key. It is universal, yet individual. It is your psyche. There is no amount of money that can buy such an element of being. In fact, abundance of material wealth would undermine its balance of nurture and nature. Being requires a choice of what you wish to give of yourself. How much of you, you wish to give to allow its consciousness.

Wherever your life has taken you so far, at some point you have steered its direction. You have been leading navigator in your own self-propagating journey of awareness. Whichever roads you ventured along, somehow, some way, you are influenced or influence. Whoever was at the helm of your ship of dreams, could it be, you created those weather conditions at any given time. Storms, whether they be insignificant or devastating, can only be endured through ourselves. Our only lens of perception is through our individuality. How we alone perceive life, its Intrigues, its threats, consequently, choose our courses of actions accordingly. Our perceiving is that mechanism, if allowed to become disingenuous, will in due course, be that conduit to attract destructive forces, physically disabling, then finally invading the psyche itself. It is possible, our individual weaknesses, as well as strengths, create our personal inner experiences of our existence.

As much as the human condition is just that, a condition, we as individuals have exceptional abilities of evolvement. Living inside a physical body has its advantages, not omitting its heavens and hells. The crux of this dilemma could emanate from our navigation of our mind-over-our-own-matter. If we believe our mind at these times of adversity, must we then believe their stories? Their mindsets are shaded and jaded with all manner of egotistical masks and monsters. They will capture, commandeer and confuse. They will save, sanctify, and strip bare all that is false, depending on their particular bias.

Power is not that which has the ability to control. Power is elements at any given time circumstances create. Whether it be wealth, intelligence, dominance, manipulation of environment, conditions of circumstances may or may not be responsible.

Our psychologic mapping might be a 'high-security deposit box' containing many priceless keys.

There is no lacking in power. Creation is that which is all.

Our choice is the deciding factor we have power to instigate at any given time in our life. When power is in place it is unstoppable. In its natural state it is a force of good for good. As its opposing force can unbalance this state, we then are given this choice of what we wish to create within this existence. Without balance no force is viable. This may feel something you recognise, or this will all be something completely alien. If you are here with me reading Orb, I am most thankful to you.

Humans, I believe, are the link that has the power to converge power and balance in this world. To foresee history is something we can perceive or pretend to control, but then this is something in the human condition and at the risk of sounding biased, humans are quite adept at creating history, not necessarily learning from it.

However, true powers of this planet are driven by nature. While seemingly invisible they give us the food we eat, the air we breathe, everything and more we could conjure up in our most imaginative dreams. Nature is what we ourselves are. If anything, we should aspire to in this life, nature stands at the pinnacle of all that is. Sadly, we have proven how our own obsessions with power continue to feed our ghosts of egos, but to no avail. They continually call for more, as they can never be content with holistic sustenance. The more ego is fed, the less the human condition becomes humane. It is as if by our hands we destroy that which we wish to create. As if this choice of acquirements will not be allowed, will not ensure nurturement and balance. Therefore, this greed for power over nature creates a dismantlement of creation itself.

Happiness is a concept we alone can create. To be of poverty or plenty, matters little in the final analysis. Life has been created for us to become an integral piece of its jigsaw. If the pieces fit, all well and good for the lucky recipient, if not, it is up to us to create a new design. Life is here for our willingness, our wishes, our wondrous abilities of creating within creation. For all the wealth in this world, you will be the poorest of souls. Our concepts of wealth constructed through the lens of greed, can only be viewed through skewed perceptions. Where there is wealth of merely materialism this could only furnish us with impermanence. To that greedy eye, impermanence may be the limit of their own spiritual depths.

Where giving of yourself is nurturing others, all life is our sea of our own humanity. Peace and security of communities. Sacredness created by our want to be this force of creation, in this 'Being Human' which is the magic we are.

I Am Here

In the visiting of the sun
I will be warmth
In the passing of the breeze
I will be breath
In the flowing of the stream
I will be nurturement
In the strength of the mountain
I will be immovable
In the depth of the oceans
I will be silence
In the eye of the storm
I will be safety
In the calling of a child
I will be refuge
In the darkness of the night
I will be the moon
In the longings of the lost
I will be home
In the fears of the abandoned
I will be rescue
In the fears of your screams
I will be calm
In the searching of your soul
I will be enlightenment
In the loss of a beloved
I will be comfort
In the eyes of wisdom
I will be understanding
In the falling of a tear
I will be compassion

In the protection of a warrior
I will be untouchable
In the famine left from greed
I will be abundance
In pain left throughout suffering
I will be healing
In the learning of how to live
I will be humility
In the choosing of how to give
I await

Forever Miraculous

Whether you are young or whether you are old
There is always something to behold
Because this world is forever miraculous

Whether you run or whether you walk
To allow time just to stop to take in the day
It just requires you to appreciate what is

People come and people go
There is always something you wish to know
Because this world is forever miraculous

If you are wealthy
Or if you are without
Understand this world is forever miraculous

Generosity stems from the heart
It is a power in which you can heal
Allowing you to see that which is real

It just requires you to appreciate your day
Life will give and life will take
This journey of sacredness we create
Discover this world is forever miraculous

Along each twist and turn
We need to love and through this learn
Humility is required to appreciate your day

If you destroy
If you create
Choosing is one for your own fate
Realise then this world is forever miraculous

There will be those who bear no soul
But believe this life is all to take
Open your heart to appreciate your day

We are all the same
We are all diverse
We live for the better
Some for the worse

Yet in the heart of us all
There is a sacred voice
It waits in the darkest souls

Forever is in our spirit
To allow your light
Will guide your way home

Be it far unto shadows fierce
Deep into dreads and doubts of heart
All will be found and carried home

To gentle light that holds your soul
Where nothing can steal that which has been forged
By that which is forever miraculous

Be Life

Now choices are in effect
You must now choose how you wish to live
It is not up to you which stone
This water of existence flows upon
The river must flow free
You cannot alter nature
Without karmic imbalance
Most are given freedom of will
Which is our nature
But we can live our choice

Then,
Be prepared to battle demons
Upon this failing
There is no other place of safety
For in this living
You may obtain wisdom
Key to set you free
Allow others to follow their own paths
If they do not wish to live in their own light
We must be humble within our sacredness
To be at peace within our hearts
Not descend into endless wars of ego

Decaying piece by piece amid their futile fight
See glimmers of foul and fleeting ghosts
Haunting without conscience
Unspoken realm of ignorance
In other-worldly inexplicableness
Our forces move to balance universes
And more there beyond
A balance we cannot adjust in our favour
Were that it ours to choose
But lies within a place of silence
Dwelling amongst sanctuary
Beyond vision lies sight
Awaiting your awareness

See then beneath life's masks
To look upon the naked face of truth
History has forged mighty paths
Where we abandoned stars
No more to shine within the darkness
Here now look above our skies
And where you see your light
Learn well to shine upon your universe
It waits within the shadows of your soul
Once found this place will nurture all
This nurturement will feed all souls

Each day is given for our giving
Be abundance of your being
Be that life filled full of living
Be completeness of all our stars
For it is We who are given

Everything Home Is

Home is our place where our molecules abide
Safe and secure
We wear it with pride
It is our comforting bubble
Floating happily inside

It shouts our names when it's time to get up
While we catch ourselves tugging the duvet
To wish ourselves a few seconds more
To ignore those bullying thoughts grinning
From behind the list of our day

Ahead awaits our converted chunks of time
Aligned to fit precisely into the jigsaw of communality
This is who we are in this larger picture of humanity
Childlike with wisdom of a thousand magi
We know what life can throw at you
But never let go of that gift of innocence

Our curtains opened to guide us out
The familiar sounds as we all shout
Nothing fills you like a jug
As hot-buttered-toasty smells
Finding our realm of kitchen
It is where we become architects
Navigators, gurus of all things scrumptious
Cultivation of our unique art of world healing
You have no idea what you are dealing
When you step into our universe

Discovering how we can create as much happiness
While being true to ourselves
In our gentle ways of quiet
But we always do agree we must be quirky
Eccentricities aside
There is code to living without taking
Where the giving of us requires a making

To create rather than decimate
To instigate powers of love
Demolish structures within our psyche
Because that is our very favourite food of life

While we all feel that last hour of work
Like a huge, heavy monster hiding
Watching, waiting
Inventing ways in which to lurk
One of us has pre-arranged
List of bits and pieces for supper's feast
Another knows where to go
For just the right kind of treats

Because by the end of this day
You can bet we are praying
To make the same difference to this earth
We are given this opportunity
To show what we are made of
To give of ourselves
To grow all our good for all our worth

You Are Loved

If you were there
When I needed a friend
You are loved more than you will ever know
If you were there when I had nowhere to go
Then you are loved with all my heart

If you were there
When I needed support
You are loved more than you will ever know
If you were there when my broken world
Fell into a million pieces
I am blessed to have known you

If you were there
When I needed the truth
You are loved more than you will ever know
You have given me compassion
When no one else would
If you were there when courage was my only wisdom
You are loved more than you will ever know

You gave me strength
When I was weak
And finding home was just a dream
You joined earth to sky
Now I fear nothing

If you were there
When I needed understanding
You are loved more than you will ever know
You opened all those foreboding places
Through your nurturements I have learnt
If you were there when all I needed was love
I have found everything I ever need
I learnt to stand and look towards the light
There I found my way beyond that lost horizon
It is I who you have allowed sight

No one could take my hopes or happiness away
Finding home was a place that I could reach
Where all things good were waiting
Where being me was more than I could dream

As you are here
I trust enough to hold out my hand
You are loved more than you will ever know
Within your heart I become a warrior
Within my soul I am a child
This earth is ours to live as one hemisphere
And now I know which way I must go

As we need to understand we are sacred shards
From that which has been shattered
We have this chance to return each sacred piece
To hold forever all that truly matters

I See Beyond This Light

Passing through the light that breathes within this dusky
silvered ivory
Truth falls upon my eyes
Immobile
I drift inside my own subconsciousness
To rise where all life has begun
Lost
But nothing unfamiliar
I cannot feel the incandescence of this sky

Where might such mighty fate and power dwell?
For all you are, you have no staircase into time dimensions
There is a place
Just out of view
Where doors of immortality await those ancient few

Walk now with seeing in your eyes
Cry and leave your soulless mind behind
Forgive the ones who treat you with contempt
They shall be forever blind
They shall be those that you will never be their kind

But I have cried upon empty hearts too many times
And all for salvation of my own
Now this once
I heeded words of wisdom
To feel no more those cruel wounds
That stole my innocence

Let me be
For I have much to give
Let me be
I allow myself to live
With light within my mind
This universe of light and love has found me
Just when darkness fell

Walk upon this earth as air
Let lift as light opens darkness
Our beauty lies within
Our destinies unfurled
Our lives owe all to life
Now we can become one

Passing through this light
I become one with all
One with day from light
One with dark
One within light
I am here with eyes
Beyond darkness
Beyond our sense of sight

If time should weary you
Look to your strength of heart
You have come too far to turn away
Whichever path you take
They all return to soul
Be that which you can give abundance

Strength of a Child

I have come to bring in the light
One step, two step, three step
I am walking through the sky
One step, two steps, three steps

I am a little child
One beat, two beats, three beats
We create rhythms with our hearts
One beat, two beats, three beats

I am a little child
One skip, two skips, three skips
I am as free as a bumble bee
One skip, two skips, three skips

Tell me Mother
What to do
When I get a little scared?
I need your hugs
To keep me safe
They keep me warm
When things make me afraid

Nothing in this whole wide world
Makes my heart grow as strong
As you with me
We are as free
As a beautiful bumble bee
One buzz, two buzzes, three buzzes

Tell me Father
What do I do
When I get a little scared?
I need your hugs
To keep me warm
When things make me afraid

Nothing in this whole wide world
Makes my heart grow so strong
As you with me
We are as free
As our gentle bumble bee
One wiggle, two wiggles, three wiggles

Although I am a child
I try to understand big things.
I wish to listen to help me grow
I wish to use my mind to see

I wish to live a nurturing life
Without need for greed
Without choice of hates
For I am born within this
Wondrous universe
Buzzing like a bumble bee
Gathering in its love

   I choose to live with gentleness

I choose to live in harmony
I can become magic
So, I can then create
Through my caring thoughts

I find my flowers every day
To share their love
In so many special ways
Child though I may be

I am understanding how to live
Life has been given
To children just like me
And I choose to learn
About everything I can

To become someone who
Will know how to teach
With other children
Who need hugs too
Then we can understand
Even though we are quite new

Our universe is here
She is waiting to nurture you
In all these funny things you do
She is smiling at us
Something I know deep inside
It is like a cosy home
I love to go live in
Those that love me

Always help me along
This is my special place
We call it nurturing
We cannot not allow
Nothing but love

Because what we have been given
Is so incredible
We do not ever wish to lose
Our magical worlds
Where we are loved
By all beautiful things
That make us grow
Like flowers for our bees
With strengths
With abilities to create
Endless possibilities

This earth's magical worlds
I wish to live within its hug
And never be afraid again
It is so very easy to be happy
It makes me full of love
Then when I am filled
I wish to pour it out
Like a jug upon our souls

Upon all fear and sadness

To make them flow away
To be washed far
Into a place of happiness
Never to return to be unkind
But leaving only good things behind

That we can help to plant its seeds
With our hearts of love
So, they will wish to grow
And then we are all able to understand
What is possible from our love
Our nurturements
Our growing every day
Together

Our world will be
Our beautiful garden of us
Like strong roots of the strongest tree
We grow our minds together
Our minds can touch the skies
We will live the best of lives

Create as we have been created
To be as wise and as kind
As we are all meant to be
It needs no wealth
Just needs you and me

Like our footsteps in the sands

Of passing time
We can leave our mark
For others who wish to walk
This place content of mind

We always leave a special mark
When we choose to give
To share a little something
Something beautiful to
Offer to this world

To stop a moment
To think
How can I make a difference
To something
To someone
To all

Some being that might have
Less than me
I can offer a crumb of my time
To see if I can make
A dark day fill with sunshine

Mother is the word I say
Or dad if he is my universe
When I need to learn to grow
The most special word in this whole world
It makes me feel safe
Then I understand
There is no place like Home

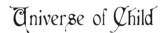

Universe of Child

To open a window to the light
No matter how small
No matter how slight
I know I never need be sad
My mother teaches me
Understand good things will come

Every day you learn how
Just little things
Little things you do not yet see
They matter to our world
And our world grows like a tree

For little wings to learn to fly
With Mum or Dad's love
Wisdom fills their eyes
I never feel alone
Because love is this place
Within my heart I forever call my home

Of all these things I do
Every day
A tiny piece of giving
I have come to learn
What it is to be alive
What is this sacredness of living

I am a child of this universe

Where all that is will nurture
Something too incredible
To allow to be ignored
I am a child of knowledge
I am a child of stars

I shall walk with all that is beauty
I will talk with many angels
It is us who are the children of this universe
That are given love beyond compare
We are those children
Who will open all doors
With our universal keys
Of Oneness with creation
Forged from strengths of earth's community

Busy lives have no time to talk
Too many things to do
Too little time to walk
I learnt from how you walked
To how you talked
I learnt from when you showed me how stuff grows
Those things that did not seem
As if they meant much at all
Explain much more than any books
I understand growing up
Is growing together

When you have so little time
To spend with me

I miss you oh so much
You that loves me
Life is far too lonely
It is never quite the same

If you would make a little time
Just here or there
For me to chat with you
For me to know you care
I understand that grownups
Have extremely busy lives
But please drip drop some time
In my special box of happy
I promise to choose the small box
That one with the lock and key
The special one
That holds my heart
There I will look after it forever
Until your next time
Then I can set it free
Time is such a mean machine
It can steal away your life
I will keep reminding you
That you can break it up
Like a big chocolate cake
And I will take a crumb or two
Whenever time gives you a break
My special days with you
Create my Universe

Within Our Mind's Eye

Some of us can see everything
We can touch the sky
Transform ourselves
So that we can fly
We can walk upon the stars
Pick them up gently
Now they can be our lanterns
Sacred lanterns to light our ways

If we never did
If we never would
Our stars would guide us
They have the powers to teach How we should live together
Although life can turn into a monster
There is always a safe place to hide
Believe when that voice in your head
Tells you to keep looking up
Telling you
That your instincts speak from deep inside
There is no need to hide
From your strengths
From your true self
All that you are
Is created from our stars

Each one will shine its light
Your heart will guide
Through your darkest days
Throughout your fearful nights
And it will be alright
When you are ready to understand
There is nothing that can harm you
The grains of sacred life
Are given to you
You need but look
And see beyond sight
It is already in your hands
Be not afraid
You are the place of warriors
All of your hopes
Each of your dreams
Are waiting for you
In shadows of your fears
They watch for your better day
And hold the gate
For your awakening
Behind the sadness
Together all will become universe

Learning to Knit

This big hole in my jumper
Where my head fits through
It is big enough for me
It is also big enough for you
Here we have a lovely jumper
That will work out we can share
It really does not matter
If we keep it here
Just as handy
For us to keep it there.
This lovely rainbow jumper
Is just made for us to wear
But if you find
The season is too warm
And such things are a bit too hot
They are so very versatile
Pop it into your cat or dog's cosy
They would love it to snuggle
As woollies make great nests
It really is not surprising
When they are knitted by the best

This box of wool in the corner
Has a multitude of colours
It can transform itself into this and that
My mum has created bobble hats
Scarfs so long they could
Go around the world a billion times
And keep everything snugly
Well keeping everything warm as toast

But you know?
When you can knit
Be sure to share a little bit
You help make this world
A better place to live
It is all about
Your willingness to give
It does not cost big monies
Just seeing what you can re-use
You can explore your local charity shops
Fling your feet across their door

And all the time
As if by magic
You are creating wondrous things
Of bringing everything together
And those things will plant the seeds
To teaching those who wish it
How to communicate
How to co-operate
How to instigate
How to illuminate
Infinite paths along which to create
From there we have abilities
We never knew we had
Incredible skills
Knitted from the love of giving
This powerful machine that generates our living
It just requires daily maintenance
From loving souls
That have the capacity for giving
Much more than they receive

They have no wish to take
As they have found the secrets
Of how life becomes richer
Through the smallest act of giving
Your choice of being
Are those pieces of caring
They are each and every stitch

This big hole in my jumper
Is big enough for me
As we share this funny old wool friend
We know we have it all
No matter if you're little
No matter if you're tall
No matter if you are a rainbow
With colours like beautiful flowers
No matter if you're happy
No matter if you're sad
To be good and caring
Is more than money will allow

More than any wealth
When you wish to learn
To be creative
You open the door
Then it is always up to you
To follow your instincts
Be more than you wished for

Just the smallest thing

Things you do from your soul
Are the biggest healers of this world
To make the smallest things
Like growing into our jumpers
We have knitted
That we can share together
To help everything
In our universe
Grow happy
Grow cosy
Grow snuggly and warm.
Because when you learn to knit
There is a whole new world to find
It just requires full attention
As much loving as you can give
No matter what life brings you
Cosy and loved is the best life lived
Love has no holes
It only fills in
That which is missing

Warrior of the Gate

Sometimes you meet a moment
Along a lonely path within your life
Sometimes you hope you find
A safe place to land
A place you wish to spend your life
When no one is there
To show you how
You can make a better day.
When nothing seems to shine
Your skies forget to light
Your morning skies
Even your dreams
Cannot find their way
A friend will always find you
Just call and hold out your hand
A friend will always find you
Look around your mind
They will be as footprints in the sand
Sometimes we believe
Life is far too dark to light
Believe in the strengths
So much strength you fear yourself
Then reach out your hand
There you will attain its wealth
When I call you
No need to fear or hesitate
I will be waiting there
I need no time
Past, present or future
For I am warrior of the gate

Mother Earth

I watched the sun go to bed
It slid down my windows
I heard it whisper
Words that echoed in my head
'Would you shine for me tomorrow
Little child of mine?'

When I watched the clouds turn grey
They dance shadows over my garden
I heard them whisper
Words that echoed in my head
'Would you shine for me tomorrow
Little child of mine?'

When I watched my sky wear its cloak
It sparkled with silvered jewels
I heard it whisper
With its gentleness
Words that melted into my head
'Would you shine for me tomorrow
Little child of mine?'

Yesterday.
When I felt our world feeling rather sad
I said, 'Please do not be afraid'
Then I heard it whisper
With countless voices
'Would you shine with me tomorrow
Little child of mine?'

Yesterday.
When I saw our world
Needing my biggest hugs
My heart grew full of love
She called me to help her heal
'Please would you shine for me tomorrow
Little child of mine?'

Today.
As I open my eyes
I have become strong as a warrior
Now can do great things
To help her in every way
I shall shine every day
I light the night stars
Because I am her universal child
For the food on my plate
I am grateful
To all those that made possible
For the clothes on my back
I am grateful
To all those that made this possible
For the wealth of good health
I have been given
With nothing expected of me
I have a beautiful world
Where I have all I need
A beautiful earth
That I wish to live within
I am so grateful
To all that has made this possible

For those who take care of me I am grateful
For this home I belong
With their love
This nurturement
Which keeps me strong
To all that has made this possible
I am so grateful
For that which I value
I am grateful
For the beautiful heart
That beats to heal our world
This love which has made this possible

For all our creators
Who enhance earth's spirit
I am grateful
For our communities of caring
Who carry the souls of life
I am so grateful
To all that have made this possible

For my heart, mind and soul
I am loved beyond compare
I give gratitude
For this day ahead
And all that I am
I will live to share
I will live to care
To be one with my universe
To be completeness
To become whole
With this Sacredness I Belong

Small Pieces of Sacredness 2

Pop the kettle on!
It's time out for that moment to reflect
Catching sight of our kitchen clock
What the heck!
Let's take a break
Before night falls
Our tummies
Begin to moan and groan
When Mum bakes us cakes
That only took a few pence
To whip up in a jiff
If we leave that pile of washing
Until after our snacks
We will be able to do a much better job
Have something tasty on the hob
And maybe even
Give our back garden a flick
If the house wand holds a grain of magic
Just let's not ease up on the power
Plug into our minds
Or we will lose the will again
That would be all too tragic
Not to mention the time!
Which is all just fine
When you have your own day
Today has worked out
Like a soft lump of clay
And it all threw us a curve ball
When our cat threw her squishy present
Halfway down our lovely cleaned hall

Which I had left immaculate
Posh polish and all
But that's life I suppose!
It's a drop in the ocean
Compared to the great scheme of things
Working together is what it's about
There is nothing like it
Grows your mind
Strengthens your body
Because life is not always what it seems
When you finally realise
Stop a while!
Open your mind's eye
There is a whole other world inside
It's about me
It's about you
It's about our points of viewing
Then melding them together
In the most wondrous ways
Like our planet and its weathers
It is sometimes scary
Sometimes sunny
Sometimes just grotty days
You cannot see those woods
For the amount of trees
But it is within your eyes
Exactly what can be seen
Back garden now looks so smart
We have given it a very large chunk
Of our time and our hearts
With the most colourful toppings
And those splendid, silvered balls as well

Sister has recycled all the odds and ends
While she was doing that
I continued to clean through our house
Nothing too fussy
Gently found a quiet place for our mouse
If she is clever enough to keep safe
From our cats
She deserves to be family
But we all feel so loved
From our collective hugs
Our House just screams
'This is your place!
This always puts
Huge smiles on faces!'
This is love
It's about how we live
It's about how we give
It's what we wish to achieve
As the rest of today
Will now give back
We have so much imagination
Words could not express
From first sounds of our new day
To last shouts of 'goodnight'!
I am only a blink away!
We are here for each other
Through the good
Especially the bad
It is all about giving
Much more than we ever had

It is not all bad
In this huge incredible universe
It is about Love
What We give out
Our Home fills with its Returnings

I Am Found

I floated away on my pillow
With a large pile of buttered toast
Saw the skies smiling at me
With a mug of hot coffee
And the night was beginning
To paint silver stars with the moon
I zoomed all around
See what could be found
With the eyes of my wisdom
Nothing would be able to miss them

There was the biggest rainbow
It was the bridge to the heavens
And I knew I was home again
Across the ocean of dreams
Incredible though this seems
All the beings of the sea
Made time to speak with me
They told of wonderful things
Angels that visit
With huge silvered wings

And I knew I was home again
There is a sacredness here
Safety for me never to fear
And I knew I was home again
Let me float on my pillow
Where I can be free

To live life so happy
Where I will know how to see
Through this world's lost horizons
On this earth's sacred sea
Of colours
Of difference
Of communities
Of wondrous
Inexplicable diversities
Of creations
Of these things in life
I choose to see
There is more to this life
I know I have found my home

Rainbow Child

Life is a colour
Not what you might think
It is unusual in its shade
Pale and yet warm
Gentle in form
Life is such a pleasing colour
Like the inside of a cloud
Is not loud!
You could say it is underestimated
And I just did!
If you think of life
As a long cool drink
On a hot summer's day
So, life has a role to play
In our day-to-day
While you're moving with the ticking of time
And that's all well and fine
If your life is without reason or rhyme
Then life would be souless

I am a rainbow child
My colours reach across the skies
To be a rainbow child
Is to speak with angels
Today I chose this colour life
It varies depending on how I am thinking
But always colours will I wear

Life is a colour that is not what you might think
Gentle in appearances
Bright
Heartwarming
Makes you feel cosy
As mysterious as the dawn
Life is such a happy shade
Like a fizzy glass of lemonade
It gives a pop
That said
And I just did!
If you chose something life-shade
You can make the link
To how it makes you feel
Love has a role to play
In our day-to-day life

While you're moving with the ticking of time
And that's all well and fine
If your life's without reason or rhyme
Check if your clock has stopped
As you may have lost your plot!

I am a rainbow child
My colours reach across skies
And as a rainbow child I speak with angels
I am a bridge of sacredness
That brings illuminations to those who wish to see
How life is this most
Beautiful of colours
We can choose to be

Then We Are Mighty

If we are all we choose to be
Then we are mighty
No matter what the cost
For only wealth is found
Within our sacredness
This realm whereupon
Our love of all that is
Shall be allowed to grow
For evermore in abundance
To live not to destroy
Or demises earth's miracles
Earth is ours to nurture
With all we are
With all we give
With all we wish
With all we live
It is ours to be those guardians
Unmoveable in strengths
While those whose beings
Take all without return
We breathe with love
We breathe with innocence
We breathe within this universe

If we are all we choose to be
Then we are mighty
No matter what the cost
For only wealth is found
Within our sacredness
This realm whereupon
Our love of all that is
Shall be allowed to grow
For evermore in abundance

Once more to shed its light
This light of nurturements
This light from our sight
Our souls gathered together
As one source of wisdom
For this
One universe we are given
Beyond horizons
Where our past has dwelled
Our present is knowing
Our future will find
The silence of our beings
And in this shard of discord
I will carry all compassions
Protected safe for when is found

You Are Here

Splinters of time pierce contentments of my mind
Haunting the haloed halls of their fortresses
Shards thrown across expanses of my thoughts
Only belief can be forged into these eyes
Sounds of past ignorance resonate like lost wisdom

I call upon my angels to hold the gate
And there without falters
All that I shall find their path
Watch the sky for me tonight
The moon will see my shadows when silence falls
We both shall meet within this place
Should time pursue my heart with phantoms?
Let witness too dreadful for mere mortals to endure
Fear not for angels guard my way
I will be at their gate before time calls future
Then all eternities command our illuminations
There I will join this bridge of hemispheres
Unto our shattered realm to heal

You are here
I know you stand so strong
Amid this tide of imbalances
We work together here
Through all life's blows and battles
You are here
While shadows hide in fear.
When time rewinds into labyrinths of wonderment
Then some shall know their way
But some may lose more than they had realised
Though you are here forevers

While those who nurtured when all was taken
Grow strengths of wisdoms
For you have sown the seeds
That have brought together this universe
Allowing this sphere's healing for our todays
Did you leave to teach someone else to fly?
I never found your note to be there to say goodbye
Was I too far away to hear your silent cries
But all that time I thought you just didn't care

I remember when you changed my world
I learnt that you were someone I could depend on
Every glance at you lifted my soul into the skies
And there I became an eagle

Although now vanished from sight
I live within your eternal energies
You walk with me amid all storms
Now I am strength itself
Walk within this universe
with Love
And now we Breathe as One

From you I came with wisdom and humble grace
From you I came while life refused a home
Denied a space to grow through love
From you my giving was all I had
From your journey I became wisdom
From each step you retraced
From you I came and smiled
In this mirror of you
My father's face

Where Love Exists

Eerily, mist descends before my inquisitive gaze. The park, our oasis within this suburban corner of planetary home, is a saving grace of my scatty, illogical, and most mystifying of minds, my local park. A place of solitude or sharing, moments offered a promise of fresh air and enrichment, a place of many guises, for countless circumstances, and thankful people.

Heavy and damp, stalking its prey inch-by-inch across each blade of grass and shrub. Fog has a sobering way of dismantling your perceptions. Those solid chunks of stability, unmoving, unimaginable. A mystery of substance, capable of dissolving, literally into thin air. Nature always explains the unexplainable I find, but not everyone appreciates such subtleties in life, or appreciates them.

Obscured as if by some magician's favourite trick, the clumpy carpet of emerald-green grass slowly absorbed by the ghoulish, ghostly air whispers away upon the ether of Friday's soft, silvered dawn. Pale and foreboding, replacing everything it smothers with emptiness, with its eraser lost only to memory.

The opaqueness of the mist creeps and crawls, seeking vignettes and impermanent structures of our social interactions. Devouring silhouettes within its consuming presence. Yet the rush and gush of the school circus has begun its deluge. Torn back, its multi-coloured spangled curtains, this big top is open to all performers of today's social entertainments or tragedies.

Assortments of shiny cars swiftly attach themselves to the slate-grey kerbs, warm and dishevelled in the chilly reluctance of Friday's dutiful hours. My magpie family have been on breakfast duty since first crack of dawn. Watching their energies, determination, nurturing of their beautiful babies, constantly fills me with wonder. They all are the most incredible testament to nature's wonders.

As the sky changes its light, a slowness sifts its sleepiness over each movement of life's clock. The week has given, and all that's left to hear are the autumn leaves drifting from the skeletal branches of trees across the park. Muffled scuffles of moist leaves punctuate the crispness of this morning's pilgrimage to the jewels of learning establishments, waiting to accept their hordes of sleepy children, willing or not to be part of their biggest picture to date.

Dog walkers cuddled in cosy colours, clumps of foliage rustling by the happiest of nosy noses. Guided by their four-legged, furriest of friends for ever, discovering new smells in their busy, canine day. Slow appreciation for each minute, by those who have learnt how to really appreciate life's pleasures. Rewinding the day's story, walking in so much love and contentment for their special angels, they know will make their lives for the betterment of every spontaneous day to come. With the last click of the clock, shuffling shoes and stifled yawns invite the coming of Home, for them, school is not a requirement. Returning home, hot snacks, treats and as it is the end of the week, just keeping snug togethers.

Almost four pm, November, days shrunken by the reconfiguration of seasons, an inevitability and brazen crack in the environment of time's landscaping.

The reconfigurations forced into the cracks of summer's weakening presence. Subtle at first, then a regularity, a familiarity of difference.

The hollowed sounds that echo back across the bowling green. Flowers vibrancies, paling as if seeping into the very blood of their earth, day by day. Rain remains prisoner of each morning's frost, transparent, transparent orbs filled with the previous night's history. Droplets of distorted images, miniaturised moments captured upon gravity-defying surfaces, injecting an air of urgency into any brisk stroll I find. Routines bordered in thick, neon, highlighters, emphasising the tedious importance of weekdays. Clothes regarding their owners as highly efficient, casual in an expensive sort of garb, just getting by attire, mishmashes, charity, that honest look eye contact that I understand without pausing for conversation.

Toby and his devoted mum appear shuffling from the green sogginess of our corner park. Each step choreographed for maximum safety. Jack Russell with copious amounts of Russell more than the typical breed, mature gentleman now, more or less blind, with a hint of deafness makes for Toby's uniqueness. I stroll with him through my eyes, listing to the one side, then the other, like a slow waltz. His timing and footwork held in bated breath and counterbalanced. The last encounter, Toby was not with his mum. I understood without need of explanation after a few lonely sightings. She, this gentle soul, in her world of single-serving micro-meals, quality brand teas and her age-old routines that gave Toby, the happiest and most Loved angel she had the privilege to share her life with. Much more of our conversing is omitted than spoken, for both our sakes. But home is a place that bears no limits I have found, for either the mind or heart. It is a place where realities meet illusions. Understanding becomes translators for all maladies, all confusions. She headed home, where all her silent memories, wrapped in eternal love awaited.

Teapot Existences of Eccentricities

Fondant, pastel colours glowing upon shiny surfaces of what is the closest any human could get to an Eden. The cracked-chocolate brick sofa imposes itself under the curved stained-glass window that nestles in our snuggle corner, always waiting for our company throughout any given day 24/7. It holds and hugs us, reassuring, safe, no demands, no icy criticism or condemnation for the criminally insane. Even the natural daylight seeps in with respectful gentleness. Warmth puffs out our soft-toned rooms, it plumps the countless colours of velvets, satins, and tactile furnishings that make our house so us. Its curvaceousness, moulding around our aches of the day, transforming our sensitive emotions into billions of happy stars. We would be utterly lost without our couch. So much emotion it holds in every crease and crevice. So much of what we are. No judgements holding our thoughts prisoners. Only reverence of atmosphere, a permanence of peace and contentment.

Not just a piece of heavy-duty furniture. No one would have believed that an unassuming lump of treated timber, reinforced nails, and brilliant carpentry skills, constructed around chocolate leather, would inevitably be responsible for virtually the complete mental health of our eccentric family. As as a result, becoming part-human, part-couch with only the most appealing of character traits.

Our purple retro-radio narrates the many hours of chits and chats
Tears and laughter with our loved and loving cats
Reading books in quirky hats
Confiding problems
Counselling friends
Watching movies making ends meet

Quite a feat of feminine strength
Keeping equilibria
Our kitchen
A place that heals all wounds
With a free cuppa too!
It chaperones home-made suppers
Mouth-watering puddings
That squelch underneath our dessert spoons
They speak all languages
They shout
You have it made!
Just taste and be transported
To paradise!
No wasting valuable together time
Clawing over the days depressing mental grime
Life is much too fine a point
Of our psychological profile
We choose not to waste such magical times
Conversing, solving problems of this world
While living in our own little swirl of paradise
It's an ability we three have
That allows us to clear away imbalances of nature
Replacing them with simplicity
Pull back the curtains of ignorance
Expose them to the sun
Of our beautiful nurturing minds
We discover the music between the lines
Of our own insanities.
Work out the melodies!
So, our universe can learn to dance
It's like the Arc de Triomphe in France
You can see your destination
From a long way ahead

Neon numbers glowing beneath the sharp, ticktocking of our kitchen clock. Twitching every second with its ticktock, out from the metal shelving and bulbous glass storage jars. Time caresses our nurturing wisdom, wraps us up like swaddling babes. There, the Aga stands protective, defying the laws of chill and misguided misery. Mum is returned from her scheduled hike around the back garden with our little darlings. Bird feeders filled, as the iced-silver moon begins to guild each shape and shadow into silhouettes. Back door bolted behind the flurried fur, fluffy pjs, giggles and jousting for best flop-out spots, to absorb the melting hours of our Friday evening. Polka-dot crockery scattered in grubby groups of love and nostalgia; bedtime tugs our reluctance to go bed, so as not to miss any home-time happiness. Heavy glances relay sinuously, silent instructions, psychic mind links developed many moons ago.

'I will take up the babies, they are ready to snuggle-in upstairs!' pierced the mumbled conversation.

'Love you, Mum!'

'You too!' sings through the house.

Journey of Returning

Three beings. One huge heart purring Infinite love
Everything welcomes us
There is a reverence
A pause of time upon within cushioned corner
Within the casement window
Full-mooned
Blood-red glass bleeds upon our weariness
As night throws its cloak across our ebbing day
Transfixed upon our flaming hearth
Night expands across our eyes
And we are heavy with all things this day
Our dreams await to take us far away among the stars
Knowing that the morning
Teapot-filled!
Our world will be all the better
For our endless stories
Snuggled in our hearts
Just ready for our returning home

Contentment Armchair

Light sifts down from this ghostly silver orb
Sky bathed with indigo-purple
Bleeding through its opaque expanse of tranquillity
As if blushing from its own beauty
I have scuttled into my room
This space
Where in any eventuality I can create
No matter how late
Or pre-break of dawn
Far too stubborn to yawn
Because in my space life becomes uniqueness
It is what you call completeness of one's being
Something in here worth seeing
Nothing materialistic you understand
But immense tangibility
You can sense its presence
But it will run through your fingers
Just like dry sand
So here is where I create
I believe it's that whole thing of fate
It will give you something special
But always add something hidden
That has the power to leave you in a state
Dissatisfaction
Impatience
Lack of self-belief
Over-sensitivity
Along with an unfailing ability of being late

I have no sense of time
That ticking, picking, persistent force
Making your mind gallop like a horse
With its unearthly battle of mind over your moment
There your head cannot rule your heart
But all the time you know you have to start
Those heart-breaking chores
Even so there is always a way
To devise ways to delay
By listening to your heart
Then you can start
Working out what stays in and what stays out
Of your busy work and play
But not good to delay
Deep sleepiness of our clock
Ticks a slower tock
Now the moon has slid across
My armchair sits resplendent in its glimmering
Absorbing the last hours of its glow
Yes I know!
My bed is so, so cosy
And I would love to go to sleep
But it can keep for a little while longer
When my will to write is less strong
And mother nature whispers
'You are stronger
My dearest child'
So, I have learnt to smile
At these aggravations
And just say 'thank you!'

For the good
For the bad
Especially all those
Happiest of times
When I could have been sad

But when they have been
It has been alright
Because that warrior in me
Always armoured for the fight
That said
I would not wish to be
That individual that pretends
Life is far too lovely
Something about living
Within the eye of these storms
It creates many scars
It moulds or cracks your spirit
And you know?
I am more worthy of my strengths
More than I would have ever believed
What I have achieved
No physicality of support
No psychological stabilities
None that I can report
Up to this point in time
I keep scavenging for discarded things
From those who have no love to give
Never wasted my time
Night-times carry me to other-worldly spheres

Past this universe of lost dreams
Beyond our moons
Where children can hold stars
And let free to realise
It is they who understand
All these meanings that others
Will not open their eyes to see
But they aren't you and me
I am home in my world of content

My Armchair Journeys

I sit, hugged as a beloved child, from a parent that knows
they have been given everything beautiful for the rest of their
life. As one whose universe is within these shadowed corners.
This is my cosy place, velvet hugs that transport my dreams
to other-worldly places, unfamiliar faces, endless endeavours
I must return to in my next visit. Questions come and go, but
now I have learnt to never ask. Strangely enough this is my
world; insanities aside, I need its oddness, it is more than a
place to visit, it is my home. My front door bears the wear of
constant hugging of our hands against its painted timber.
Returned from work, or the end of a draining, occasionally
self-sustaining working day.

That leaves you completely fractured
Like a delicate piece of pottery
Because life is this human-tide of lotteries
Do you wish to belong?
Or override your instincts
About our human-race
You could be wrong
But honestly
You can feel it in the muscles of your face
Whether your energy levels are up to lying today
Where hurts have come and gone
My armchair is this shape where I belong
And nothing can harm me here
It is my cosy armchair
Where I can sing
Where I can dream
Where I can become inexplicably insane

So that my eccentricities are catered for
And everyday life?
It is all about those priorities
If you do not take responsibility
You run the risk of wasting
The fundamental laws of time
And there my whole world makes perfect sense
No pantomimes
Dramas or ugly pretence
I know where the river flows from my little pond
At any given time
I know where it ends
And just between friends
That's exactly how I like it
There is another law
This one resides in my mind
Stating there is only one way to be
For me that is
Being a nurturing force
The only way I wish to live
All about the giving
Being kind finds all those missing pieces
Of innocence
That could otherwise have been overlooked
Like a book from a friend
Left on your shelves
Waiting for you to take it
To your cosy armchair
Fall inside its pages

It could take you ages
To reach the end
But time cannot replace
Or replicate a friend
Some things are so unique they defy comprehension
I see it more now than I have ever seen it before
While the chores of the day have been completed
Smug takes over my face
Yes, I can honestly say
This is where I wish to return tonight
And all nights that return me home
To my flickering fireplace
Warm, toasty hands
Around my mug of hot chocolate
And some hot buttered toast
I fling myself into my space
I am here
This sacred place
My inner space
Of balance
All things lovely
For my self-awareness
Life just becomes its best-ever version of itself
You know when some things are sacred
When everything you are has given its best
It is all about priorities you see
Through that opaque door
Where life is as nowhere else
Home is always this place
Where I always am
One special place
Where my insane mind can rest
In the scheme of life

It is a complex equation
To agree with notions
Of our advancement in intelligence
To sum up this would be
Only a vague approximation
Of good and bad
What makes the best in me
I have no such intent
I really wish I had
As a species we have profound abilities
To create alternate realities
To build
Fashion
Influence
Sustain life-enhancing systems
Environmental layers of communication
As well as community evolvement
This in itself to generate endless possibilities
For all life's species
This can instigate infinitesimal possibilities
New concepts of life
That will then have access to
Create its own day and night
It is our combined abilities
Insights!
Positive energies
That will bring this force of nature
Into the ultimate convergence
Of all we are meant to be
In order to become guardians
Of this sacred Orb
Foundations of what we are
As a species of worth

Require our abilities
Of empathic nurturement
Becoming willingness to merge ourselves
With that which is in need
Becoming its energy source
Becoming its roots
From which it can gain sustenance
On all levels
Life is never a one-way street
Whatever is given
Shall be returned
Universal laws are in effect
Nature's effectiveness
Nature's oneness
By you allowing your true-self
Its freedom of being.
Love and all that love creates
Is our universal mother
She is the giver of all that is
In this absoluteness of life
She cannot allow destruction
She is the ultimate warrior
Our existences are her legacies
Our choices give us knowledge
This sacred knowledge of how to live

It is through her that we are allowed
To breathe
It is She that gives us sight to see
It is She that finds us when we fall
It is She that forgives us
When we choose to fall

At our wanting more
We allow others to live less
All the while knowing so much
Still unable to feel nature's touch
To pour our souls into another's heart
Is to have sacredness in ours
Becoming all
We become universe
In this becoming
We can let in the knowledge
Out of this Orb of Hemispheres
While broken pieces will remain
You only need open your heart
Mind shall become creations
From your soul
From your light of consciousness
This depth of being
You create this power to see
Where all your confusions
Are as mists upon oceans
Of insignificance
To be as oneness
Is to create within your integrity
It requires nothing but your love

Upon my dreams of home
My armchair awaits to hold my heart
To cradle me as her child
We will speak together
In this place where all are loved
In lands where time is but thought
Thoughts of wondrous ways of being
Of what we can be

Within our earthen sphere
If we believe we can fly
Beyond all realms
Each day will take us everywhere
Here we can allow
Our hemispheres to come together
To heal this sacred sphere once more
We have arrived at our clock
To be those who can create
This time of healing
As we awake to grow
Humble in our ways
Our earth will breathe
Our earth will receive
Our love in all its forms
As we become aware
This oneness will take us there
When our understanding
Will create lights of consciousness
We will hear its calling
Hemispheres awaiting
Our time of healing
Together we can believe
That we are universal

I Ask of You

Look at me
I am a child
Please help me to grow up good
There is so much to learn
But with wisdom
And my willingness
To learn humility
I wish to create my place in this world

Please listen
I am a child
Help me to grow up good
There is so much to learn
But with wisdom
And my willingness
To learn with Humility
I wish to create
Such a good place in this world

Hear me please
I am a child
Would you help me to grow up good?
There is so much to learn
But with wisdom
My willingness to earn
My beautiful place
In this Beautiful World

Understand me
I am a child
Would you grow with me
To grow up good?
There is so much to learn
But with wisdom
Such is my willingness
To create my place in this world

I am this child
Your timeless child
Through your love
I am all.
Watch over me
Keep me close within
I will learn the best
Within good times
Throughout all bad
I see my path ahead
It always returns to you

I am a child
Help me evolve
I will be ready to grow up good
With all your nurturing
I will be all I can
And become more
From the love of you
There are always lessons
I have your wisdoms
I choose to be all the good that I am
This is all I ask of you

Journeying to Difference

I love to go on a journey
My feet feel like wings
They tip and tap
And I can clap
To the rhythm of their beat
When some days get me down
My face won't make a frown
Because I am going on a journey
With loves and hugs
To keep me safe and sound
I love to go on a journey
My heart feels as happy
As a bird I am free
And I can clap
To the rhythm of my beat
When some days get me down
My face won't make a frown
Because I am going on a journey
With loves and hugs
To keep me safe and sound
I love to go on a journey
My heart just flies like a bird
So high up into the sky
My heart feels so happy
No more times to cry
When some days get me down
I refuse to make a frown
Because I am going on a journey
With loves and hugs
To keep me safe and sound

Because of you
I know my way
I have learnt so well
How to make a wonderful life
For I am making such a difference
In this Beautiful World

Your Light Home

In this returning to our past
We are walking through its ashes
But we are afraid to look
At all the broken pieces that it took
To arrive at this place
It is hard to recognise ourselves
In a time where we have learnt so little
We can create so much
Plant fields of crops
To feed ourselves
Then feed the world
Communicate in outer space
Understand our meanings
Or so we hope
By watching each other's face
But there is something lost
Something important gone
Without a trace?
If this is a race
Who is winning?
I have been looking at the daily news
So much I would wish to choose
To teach a child how to be a role model
What I am so perplexed to find
Understanding the human mind
There is nothing as yet
I have found
That keeps my feet
Firmly on the ground
More than the innocence of a child

Just a little smile
When sleepiness has melted
Into limbs that refuse to rest
When time has stolen
All those things you had planned
Tomorrow is another day
Or so they say!
I would give every grain I am
To carry that box of answers
Answers to the why's
To the where's
But most importantly
What does it take to care?

I am those
I am the wishing
Who give of their lives
To build all that it takes
To live together here and now
Those who give their hearts
And share their souls
For the good of this world
Without fear or greed
Without hate or false intentions
Without ignorance or abandoned will
Without needs of the ills
Of what ego breeds
For I am those
I am the wishing
Who give of their lives
For I am Warrior

For I am those
I am the fallen
But I am the strength of all
I am the strength
Of those who have been before
And I will stand this gate
Beyond all time
It is of those
Who give of their hearts
Who share of their souls
For the good of this world
Without fear or greed
Without hate or false intentions
Without ignorance or selfish will.
In returning to our pas
We are walking through our ashes
But in the fear
We failed to see our strengths.
Now time to understand
This earth has allowed to us
It is our hemisphere of enlightenment
To learn from our children
How to create together
Create the dreams
We can allow to live
This earth has given all that is
Here is where we learn from our children
How to grow together in its light

They open doors of sacred realms
Truth shines in your eyes
They see where light dwells
Questions are all answers
In the blink of your mind's eye
There is nothing to fear
You are your own spirit
Be everything and more
To see where we can grow
As forests we will nurture
This universe
So wondrous as to touch the sky
And as we grow together
We can dream within our beauties
And reach sacredness itself
Within our souls we will have grown
Mighty forests of our dreams
With every choice
Through every voice
We allow this sun to shine
Upon each footstep
Upon each new path
Our children will find their way
They will be enlightenment
For those weakened
For those broken by their wounds
Our fearless child will be
Be of armour of sacred life
Be of your worthiness
Be good force from your own light
Be that beacon through our night
To see their way back home
To find our way back Home

Tom's Seahorse

Today was bound to arrive. Tom's inexplicable day. It was of
no surprise to me, knowing Tom as the angel-soul that I
know him to be. So it is, in the whole history of histories, this
day would find its way to Tom. We had watched over Tom
for the whole entirety of his life, his uniqueness of spirit
called us into his realm, and so we have come. Wherever
spirit of soul is of a particular eccentricity, you might say,
spirit of this soul appears to us, so we are then able to work
as one entity, to protect and nurture this evolutionary being.
Today we warriors have seen all these nurturements, all this
selflessness, all that is both sides of our hemispheres, these
convergences of Tom.

Tom knew today would be an incredible day. Something
had snuggled itself inside a part of his head, only reserved
for the happiest of thoughts. You know that private mind
compartment specially reserved for those things you have no
idea what to do with, where to file them, under which
categories, and where on earth they end up once there.
Importantly though, many would agree, is the fact that they
possess an incredible homing instinct just at those needy
times in our life's memories which are, without a doubt, *the*
most mystical elements ever (in the world of veers) given to
us. My belief also, is that memories are allowed all beings on
this planet, irrelevant of size, shape, make-up, or
temperament.

In Tom's world everything is relevant, everything matters.
There is nothing, nothing at all (in the world of nothings)
given to us, that does not go unnoticed, unloved or un-
nurtured by Tom. This is Tom we are talking about, Tom is

a force of nature unlike some, and likened to those with souls of angels.

When he had slipped into the cosiness of his bed last night, from his busy working week, he knew this weekend would be waiting for his magic to help heal all the hurts of this world.

Sleep had conjured up a fantastical dream, only special dreams such as that invariably opened the doors to a very special day ahead. Tom knew only something inexplicable was about to happen today, waiting to step out from underneath a familiar object or communal garden fixture, too ordinary to be of any significance. But for reasons unbeknown to the kindest of souls, something was stuck to Tom, like a splat of spaghetti sauce on your best woolly jumper; as much as you wipe it off, you know it is still with you.

This was a day waiting for Tom to step into, like an old familiar pair of jeans that had travelled many exciting journeys, and always felt as if they created good times, as if by time travel.

Sleek and glossy stood a kayak, slightly leaning into the busy corner of Tom's colourful, cosy bedroom. It was a large bedroom as bedrooms go, everything had a look about it that gave you the impression that it most certainly had a story to tell and Tom had the knack of making stories as easily as if he was a magician.

Soft, gentle rain drizzled down upon the invisibility of the big bay window that allowed Tom a panoramic view of the coastline. A cheeky smile began creeping across his face.

'Saturday! It's Saturday, I love weekends!'

The alarm pierced the peaceful air that coated the entire contents of a room much loved and much nurtured. As if plugged into a charger, Tom's eyes opened to the second buzz of his soft, green chunky, alarm clock.

The duvet flung across with a flourish, as if to say, 'this is my day, where I make good things happen!'

In the blink of an eye it seemed the time tunnel of showering, dressing and, in this case, taking-pride in one's appearance, not to mention home-world, was all achieved with such speed and spectacular precision there was something rather other-worldly at play, in the realms of other worlds.

Room fluffed-up and freshened ready for a return of a fabulous warrior to his beloved castle. As it happened, everyone at home was not at home. Holidays crept into the household by the end of yesterday, because Friday being chosen by the wise and weary, mum and dad essentially, would work out the most sensible day of the week to run free. So then, house empty apart from Tom's splendid cat, who he would have you know, is the most amicable, loving and intelligent feline known to the whole knowledge of human existence and far, far beyond. As a kitten, would sleep on the huge, fluffy bean bag at the bottom of the bed. These grown-up days, nothing less than his status demands, so it's Tom's bed, when the mood takes, or quite the connoisseur of lounge and luxuries, the soft, green, leather armchair next to the log burner built into the opposite corner at an angle, just to maintain his laws of quirky. But we, as guardians of such a beautiful soul knew even Tom's cat, especially Tom's cat, was to be magical.

Sky on a bright, sunny morning would usually consist of a blueness so blue as to be incandescent to the eye. This sky, however, had been especially blended into a delicate shade of green, so delicate that it would never be detected.

It was to honour Tom, his favourite colour, and so as this day was to be special in Tom's nurturing world all things Tom would be sprinkled into each and every sparkle of each and every moment, without the slightest of discoveries. Though somewhere, in the far distant universes these sprinkles of love would have significant meanings in the world of meanings.

Once breakfast had been assembled with all the thought and gratefulness as was usual, music from the resident, egg-yellow radio danced around the fresh fragments from rusty-brown toasts and pungent, ground coffee, and that was just fine for Tom's weekend-morning world. While some mornings can come and go, pass as if they were of no consequence at all, days, nights, life in general had special meanings to Tom. Fruits were an essential ingredient within the breakfast recentring. All elements that were needed to build that bridge from Tom's other-worldly, night-time being, across to the contrasting worlds of our day-life and the challenges they bring. Fruits are where the line is drawn in granite, and so some important things should be so.

Time on the big, industrial kitchen clock stared at Tom, 'Out and about time, Tom!' Somewhere close-by a little bay sat waiting for its familiar and loved moment of serenities and solitude with his presence. Hours would drift by, long before any other humans would dream to venture out into this place of sacredness. Softly an engine purred out of the drive with an unmistakable silhouette of a sleek, red kayak strapped to the roof of a sage-green and ivory VW camper van. Sunbathing in the sand-strewn floor of the front porch lay a handful of multicoloured flip-flops and a spare cooler box stacked with citrus shades of beach towels.

The shelves there carried copious selections of suncreams, along with a rainbow array of water flasks and healthy grains and nut snacks; yes, all such as Tom are well aligned with this particular world, you could say.

Somewhere, never too far away, the infinitesimal chemistry, choices, along with the innate alchemy of our Tom's existence are being nurtured in an unseen realm. There protected through and throughout a most marvellous universe, a universe known to Tom, but as in dream, silent and surreal, as to exist within spirit as, what humans call instinct. It is one thing to have a thought about something that haunts our memories, strange or suspicious it may be, we can choose to cast it aside. Instinct, you might agree, is something ephemeral, a something adhered to your psyche with its own life force. Therefore, this oddity of spatial awareness that is Tom's life, is in full illumination of that which cannot be explained, by those who live within the blindness of their own shadows.

Sapphire blue sparkled across Tom's line of vision, as he turned into the warmth of the bay's greened-greys rock formation. It looked as if they had opened up their huge, granite arms and scooped in the shimmering waters to keep safe for those who wished to find their little place of sanctuary. Camper parked in a tiny niche, out of direct sunlight beneath a deep overhang, 'Magical, just for me,' Tom would whisper to himself as he pulled up the brake. Unpacking would be a case of grabbing a towel, well-worn backpack that had travelled to most destinations that had bodies of water as their geographical make-up dictated. Water is Tom, as sky is air, indistinguishable from each other.

Nothing unnecessary was any part of this plan of action; kayak was priority, anything else was and is a bonus. Leviathan of early morning's tides and tranquility's long ship of weekend sanities, with the promise of new adventures to forge within mind, body and soul. Only the basic of basics fell into the rucksack, anything else would stay in the camper van, it was always so good going back, re-strapping the kayak, then slipping into the front seats to snack and absorb that morning's contentment. Listening to music blending together all the loveliest memories in Tom's kaleidoscopic mind. To say this is a character of eccentricities is to ask, 'Do you wish to live a happy life? But of course!'

Today had an unusualness, something Tom was meant to encounter, in an unassuming sort of way. From the minute his forever-worn flip-flops hit the sand, towel hurled into the long-boat, there fell a reverence, an intense presence of peace and contentment, never felt in quite this way before. Long, slow, flowing strokes of the smooth, slender paddles, scooped into water, as if to crack the surface of a sapphire-blue custard. By now the sun's iridescence had gilded everything the eye could see. Out and out, Tom guided his water-horse, only them both in the whole of this sea of Tom and tranquility keeping not too far from the coast's rustic and rough charcoal rock formations, as to navigate with a sense of safety. The tide nudged, gently, with a reassuring rhythm, like a rocking chair. As one of the little headphones fell out Tom suddenly felt quite strange. Removing the other, it seemed all sound, sounds from anywhere, the birds overhead, the oars, the water, vanished. Pulling the oars back into the boat, there came a soft, humming sound.

One of those moments when you do not believe what you are really hearing, as most of us have experienced. But this funny, little, happy sound was something so different, that you really wanted to know it was being picked up by your senses, it was as real as you were, as real as reality appeared to be.

'Zwee! Zweeeaaah! Zwee! Zweeeaahhh!'

Such an unusual sound, it could not be anything familiar as Tom realised, nothing familiar in the whole history of familiarities he surmised.

'Zwee! Zweeeaaah! Zweeee! Zweeeaahhhhh!'

Holding still, focusing downwards into the glints of pure sunlight sparking from the flowing mountains and chiselled canyons of the seaweed-green waters, pausing his eyes downwards, beyond the sea's cascading crests foam and fluid forms. There, there, in amongst the mesmerising jades and jarring shapes distorting, deceiving the mind's eye, an unmistakable shape. Tom felt himself leaning towards this form, such a little form, but so beautiful, perfect in its symmetry, he held his breath so as to not scare it away, not even create a possibility of losing this incredible moment forever. This moment he knew, would be a once-in-a-lifetime moment.

Seahorse? It is a seahorse! As the softest, most soulful eyes stared back, as if mesmerised by Tom's arrival at this place, at this particular time, by this particular individual.

'I have come to meet you, Tom!'

Tom held his breath, in the hope he might snap himself out of this daydream, this slip into another state, could it be a hypnosis, brought on by the movement of the waves, burnished bronze from the zenith of the sun's rays?

'Yes! You are not dreaming; it is I, Tom! Everyone calls me Shard, everyone in my world that is.'

'That is a fine name, may I?'

'I would be honoured, Tom!'

'But how do you know my name?'

'You know, we just do.'

'We?'

'Us, we,' explained Shard. 'Us that live in the depths of this sea. Us that watch all that mankind does and is doing every day.' Now Tom was holding onto the sides of his kayak, realising he and his boat were being carried along by a rather strong current that began just about the same time as Shard appeared.

'Please excuse us, Tom, we need to take you to our little "bay of illusions" that is not a bay at all, but a fantastical cave, where we, all of us are then able to speak with you.' In an instant they were there. A cave of epic proportions, its rock formation arched above forming a sky encrusted with sparkling jewels that, once again, mesmerised Tom. He was aware of countless beings of all shapes and sizes watching, waiting for this sacred assembly.

'As you are adapted to be land dwellers, we, as you know, are likewise adapted to live within this great ocean.

'But as you are aware, there is a change happening. This change is cause for much concern within our oceanic world. Where once we all grew, lived and sustained the very heart of this universe, within our universe. Infinitesimals abounded, we, us, looked after each other for the good of all. Of late, the change has descended throughout, affecting endless beings that inhabit our home. Now it has brought with it many dangers, dangers we, us, are not able to undo.

'We have spoken with all the other-worldly inhabitants within spheres of this world, our world.'

Voices were drifting around this amphitheatre of ancient rock formation, formations that had taken countless years to come into existence. This, and all these magical worlds were given to us from the very beginning of time itself. Tom knew this moment was magical. Languages were being spoken by endless incredible beings. Then Tom held silent, these some familiar, some never seen before beings, were speaking to Shard. 'It is Shard who is translator!' the silent voice shouted through Tom's mind.

So many sounds, sounds Tom recognised, some never heard before. A family of whales drifted forwards, into the centre of the purple-blue lagoon that was centre stage of this place of togetherness. They, a family of four, two babies, mother and father, spoke of their continuing battle to keep from humans. How their waters have been so badly spoilt they witness the daily struggles and sorrows of all that it affects. Their two babies held on to their mother tightly, as she cried bitterly. As their father continued, he explained the greed of human condition, how this had gradually harmed all of our earth in ways far too numerous and terrifying to bring to voice, but that he understands. Tom knows this voice of all, unbeknown to him he had heard these voices many times as he slept. They had all spoken to him in his dreams over so many years. A strange light shone through the cave, a light that held onto every being within the gathering of souls. Dissolving into the lagoon in this great temple of minds, silence arrived, everything could speak to each other without speaking. Tom knew sometime, somehow, he knew this place from a child.

Shard looked over to him. This was his place where he would come in times of need, his safe place.

It was then Tom did understand more than he ever thought he knew. Every being in this gathering had connected with Tom's psyche. Thoughts, feelings, experiences, hopes and wishes were flooding through Tom's mind. They had all become one sacred universe of being.

Myriads of fish, infinitesimal of size, species, but with one voice. Their lives were being destroyed by this all-consuming unconsciousness. Humans, it seemed, had now chosen to take, rather than give. Take from beauty. Take from earth's wealth of nurturements, from its very sacredness, to fill their greed. However, no matter how much they take, there is no way of filling up their wants. Life cannot be stolen, abused, or abandoned in order to restore that which has become distorted by egos. This human condition is of our choosing, is of our willingness to undo that which is a sphere of eternities. In being so, it has power to give and power to take. As allowed, within the realms of mother nature, balance is the sacred pendulum. She will regain or restore as she sees fit. There all that is will be brought into balance, restored and nurtured to attain the highest evolvement. Man has deemed his will upon mother nature's realm, without understanding of the inexplicableness of their own lives, their own world in which they live. They have chosen to exist in the shallowness of their own minds. Instead of becoming their own mindscapes of infinities, they now chain themselves to their own ignorance and the abundance of the limitations that brings.

Time stood still, as in these moments of inexplicabilities time has no meaning, therefore, time becomes suspended as to allow sacredness.

Colours of deep oceans, bled into the morning brightness of orange-peaches that opened up full expanses of sky, as if to transport you wherever you wished to go. Tom realised his whole day had returned to the edge of dusk. It was time, in the human-world, to make his way home.

'Yes, time now, Tom, we will return you home safely,' Shard whispered.

As Tom turned his head, Shard was smiling contentedly at him. There was a feeling of complete warmth and happiness like never before. When Tom opened his eyes again, he could hear his favourite band playing on his psychedelic-coloured radio he was given by his best friend, who would be in his life foreverness. He smiled, a strange and quizzical smile, discovering he was transported back home, kayak and all.

'Goodnight Tom!' shouted his mum. 'The strangest thing! I found that necklace you bought me when you were in school, Tom. You remember? The beautiful silver seahorse. It was just lying on that book I bought you, our favourite bay where you spend so much of time in that funny old boat of yours. Did you find it and put it there? Yes! Of course you did. There was a puddle just on the floor below it, I know you and your bare feet. You would live in the sea if you could, always knew you would be a water baby.'

A large hot cocoa, alongside a stack of hot buttered grained bread sat on his bedside cupboard that he had made from a pile of cherry boxes his friend had given him, as she knew he loved upcycling anything time would make possible.

His bed lamp was a BMW headlight, which he fitted into a Perspex box, lined with multicoloured lights. The other of the pair sat on a shelf in his work corner, inside its rather soothing racing-green Perspex casings. With the soft tick-tocking of his surf clock, the room held a feeling of change. The half-light from the lamps cast strange shadows around Tom's cosy room. But within his heavy sleepiness, the crunch of fresh bread, bathed in butter, sounded sifted like sand, throughout his heavy-eyed thoughts. Memories began floating around his recollections of his happy day. Friday, this off down to his bay weekend, had been like no other. In the haze of scrummy hot chocolate and half-light memories Tom knew something special had happened today. Something unique in the world of inexplicabilities. Something he was part of, in that being part of there was something only he would know how to translate in this hemisphere. Was it coincidence that I was exceptional in school at languages? Why is it I am an exceptional swimmer? All I have ever wished to be is a naturalist. Now I am living my dream, working in all ways possible to find ways of creating, sustaining and nurturing this earth, this world where everything can live together in balance, where we, as a race become nurturers, learning how we return ourselves to the sphere we are meant to be. In this moment Tom knew this was exactly what he was meant to do, on his direct journey towards his purpose in this hemisphere.

With the last sip of cocoa, Tom realised today, his day, was that day that had waited for him. It had always waited. In the span of time, we call a lifetime, events happen to us. Whether we wish them or not, some things require certain individuals to travel far beyond this mind hemisphere within their span of life. Only they can choose.

Slowly the last waking blink cradled Tom's dreams. Other-worldly adventures were about to transport him across his universe. Tom had only begun this Friday's unusual journey. Fridays, I have found, are always different. One thing for certain, Tom's world would never be the same again.

Some journeys await those who await.

Togetherness

Then we were three
You brought into this world
To bring in your love
Me blessed with you
To nurture with angels
Sent here from above
Today we are three
Shining our light in this world
Our hearts bring only love
Being blessed with you
I journey with angels
That visit here from above
Now as we three
Grow as one in this world
With strengths we grow only love
From our blessings together
We walk paths with angels
When they light our ways with love
Our lives for us three
Become journeys of discovery
As all we are nurturers of love
Humility smiles upon our souls
Here is this place where we behold angels
Now we are three
We inspire and illuminate this world
As you created mother earth with infinite loves

To understand how much we are forever blessed
We three now understand why there are angels
And how we can become their light with our love
Being together to share our light
We are as stars illuminating darkness
Our lives are sight in allowing understanding
Together We Are Endless Lifetimes

Night-time's Notions

There is a dressing gown
On my bedroom floor
Which should be hanging
On the back of my bedroom door
On its peg
That says
'This is where I belong!'
But I cannot get out of bed
Because I am so tired
I am looking around
Seeing everything I need
And you never let me down
Because of your
Cosy colours
I have just found
Enough energy to move around
It feels so much better
That I just might use
This 'trick of the light'
To help me diffuse
Light through my eyes
Then find how to move my limbs
In many other ways
It camouflages the mess
From the weekend's madness
Use it as fun-house effect
Colours are the music of my room
Illusions of being well-kept
All distractions

And all the while
I can laugh and smile
When Mum appears at her unexpected moments
Instead of feeling like I am a lazy bones
I can hold my head high
Saunter in with my rhubarb pie
You will never imagine such happiness!

There is a dressing gown
On my bedroom floor
I know it should be hangin
On my bedroom door
But life is far too short for
Sweating-the-small stuff
In any case
Tonight, I will make it all good
When I return to read my book
Wish for all beautiful things
To find me tomorrow

Achievements of Alchemy

As children most of us lived every day in the hopes of creating happiness, of happiness being created within our lives. Facts of circumstances are secondary, even lost amidst abstracts of infancy, innocence, and insufficiency of earth-time. If a child uses time wisely, possibilities of nurturing guidance are then possible. Paths of enlightenment become illuminated by those very orbs of knowledge they themselves allow into this world, through their love and nurturement.

It is these paths that are illuminated with infinite orbs of knowledge for greater good, both to oneself as well as others. Time abused without care or compassion will, as its legacy demands, tear apart all that has created existence itself. There is no means of recentring, individualities of healing elements become detached, wounded, abandoned by ignorance determined by destructive mindsets. Those who choose to tear apart from nature and its nurturing hemispheres submerge their natural instincts of nurturement. Both sides of their hemispheres of spirit are then lost to each other. Our choices are guided by our innate wish to create happiness and in turn be happy. Fears, and their legacies of discord, attach themselves to elements in the psyche that are lacking completeness, self-belief, sense of strength of one's own self and its sacredness waiting to nurture and protect all life within this sacred sphere.

As children most of us lived our lives with the hope that we can make a better difference during our daily life.

By just being there, instinctively knowing that our lives have been given to us, so that we then will understand that this day is our unique chance to give our gift of our individuality back in return. Not as a matter of pride, not as a matter of ego, not as a matter of greed, but as a being aligned with their nature of balance and abundance. Wisdom comes throughout passing of time. Time's healing light bathing the infinite plains of human emotions, as a life-enhancing friend. That other part of you that feeds your spirit whenever needed. No need of speech, communication on such levels speaks in a far more powerful language. Through living and dying along your corridors of existence, wisdom finds you in amongst your own devastation, and reaches in to pull you out. If you wish it, the remnants of your ego can be forged to then be indestructible in their nature. Alchemy is achieved. There is no loss, for loss creates a deficit of spirit. There is only abundance through your ability to nurture from that which was desolate or detached from its authentic self-achievements always do require our beautiful skills of alchemy.

Forces of Alchemy

Abundance is to become earth's completeness
Where love is Held
Given with all and more
There is no loss
With all and more
There are no abandonments
Where love is
Planted with integrity
There is no desolation
Where love is
Nurtured with heart and soul
There will be no ignorance
Where love is
Protected with strengths of warriors.
There are no fears
Where love is
This vehicle with all that wish to journey
There is no confusion
Where love is
Lie the paths you wish to choose
Where love is
You are all you wish to be
Without doubts
Without fears
Where love is
All knowledge remains

Until we choose our destination
That will take us over that bridge
Where love is
It cannot be lost
Only found
Love can never die
While knowing this love
Incomprehensible
Beyond complete
When some have not
There is this power of
Something beyond ourselves

When I am stumbling around
I can see your light
Then I know
That is where Love is
Unlock our hearts to freedom
For all we may have created in this world
We are but children of our universe
Here through its grace and favour
But it is we that need to walk with wisdom
As to share our light upon those in darkness
To lift their eyes from pain and inhumanity
Where love is
Is within the air we breathe
Where love is
Weaves the tapestries of our lives
That we work together
With one dream
With one belief
With one universal community

I Write

I write this book
For those who wish integrity
In ways only they will know how
I write this book
For those without hope or hate
In ways only they can survive somehow
In those days when hurts won't wait
Without fear or fearsomeness
Where it seems, all is lost
Where being with some
Can be much worse than being alone
Behind your eyes
A place scarily darker than
Your nightmares have ever been
This was never to be part of your dream
And it is not OK
You did not realise your stars could not be aligned
There was no time to mend the scars
No one told you
That your elements could not be combined?
Now your molecules and DNA are too complex to refine
And it is not OK
When our planets collided
Nothing had been nurtured
The ground on which you walked divided into jagged pieces

Your space is abandoned
Good energies blown away
Into peace-meal-parcels
Of disappointment
It is far too tough a call to say
Who then am I?
To dare write these words?
Written without ego or delusions or ingratitude
Illuminating shameless shadows
Uncovering viscousness
Of life within the stagnant spheres of greed
Fast-flowing rivers of insatiable
Intolerable
Infestations of misdeeds
All in the name of progress
Here is where I need to digress
Because it is really not OK
Ravenous
Consuming and devouring needs
Emotionless hearts
That pour their poisons
Onto innocence
Left to bleed
Who am I to say?
But one thing for sure
I know my way
Into my soul
Flowing from our sacred waterfalls of instinct
Replacing them with foulness of rotting insecurity

Mindscapes of self-serving shadows
Wraiths of darkness
Illusions that seek out our doubts
To feed upon that which has survived
Without conscience
But for the lie
This face of deceit
Staring at us whenever we meet
Across our great divide of consciousness
Last battle forges the sword
Or creates the Uniqueness
Of our oneness

Children of the Phoenix

As night ascends her moon unto our skies
I see her silvered orb reflected
Incandescent upon our souls
When all life's beauty
Rests in splendour unsuspecting.
Your innocence of beauty can no more
Be as mist beneath the dawn
For sacredness has come to keep safe
There shall to grow
Strong and mighty
Loved so beloved
Never more be fearful
Never more feel such pains
Or fall abandoned to hate or harm

Child of the Phoenix
You have risen from ashes of the brave
Each day you give
These contents of your soul.
When all that you are is shattered
You rise again
You breathe forevermore.
And all these shards of love
Align to show us how to live
We wait for your light
To shine unto our eyes
Then we will know you are there

Within the darkest storms
Throughout earthly mantled skies
Within this impermanence
Returning as tide upon the shores
For all you are is sacredness
Where moon returns to night

Eternal Gatekeeper

Bright is the light that emanates
From a heart of love
Bright is the light that shows
This good of us
Giving all that you can give
Is more than wealth bestowed

Giving all that you can live
Is your wisdom
To be a place of tranquillity is where your soul belongs
Where all majesty abides
Is where nature heals all wrongs
And in this inexplicableness
We are those who find our way
To this sacredness place of angels
Where mighty deeds are done

Through darkest times
Held fast by warriors
Where others would fear and run
Bright is the light that emanates
From heart of love
So bright this light
Will show the good of us
And yet we can be
These that will not harm
Fire upon our steel
Shall make us stronger

There within this
Make pain our steel
That holds our light
To make us calm our beings
There upon your way to journey
See those who are lost upon their paths
There be that one
Who opens gates of sanctuary
Allowing this your being
To enter all that surrounds
Your love
Thereupon your spirit
With all your hearts.

Journey of Knowledge

Ready for school today?
Where you will teach your teacher
Your wisdom when you say
'I am learning how to be a great individual
While growing with humility every day?'

Ready for school today?
Where you can teach your teacher
Some of your wisdom when you say
'How can I become a great individual
While growing with humility every day?'

So, am I ready for school today?
Where I could help my teacher in some way
Could I make some time to be a strong grown-up?
It's sometimes too hard to be responsible
And I get scared when life leaves me sad

Will I be ready for school today?
I know you give me so much strength
When life becomes too confusing
'Will you hug me when I am feeling sad?'
I don't know why nothing makes sense

I helped make ready for school today!
Rucksack ready and clothes so smart
I will never have to be afraid
Because now I understand how strong you are

You show me how to live
You show me how to give
You shine upon my world
Now I can find my way
Along your path of light
Here we will journey onwards
Growing up Together

Crumbs!

The crumbs in the bottom of my lunch box
Lie waiting to make some little being smile
They always fall off my bits of cake
They flake and break
Then I have more than I did before
Because that is what life gives you in return
Then all your stars will light your way
You will know how to shine!
Big foods were never made for one
And you know what?
I never wish to discard them in a bin
Not even some
Seems so wrong
Not right at all in my scruffy book!

The crumbs in the bottom of my lunch box
Lie waiting to make a little being smile
They always fall off my bits of cake
They flake so I can share
Just to feed nature's friends
My mother? Father? Helps me
Looking after little beings
Reading stories to the trees
My crummy lunch box has taught me
What it means to be at one with this earth
And this is how I intend to stay
When I eat my sandwiches
There is always some being that needs a meal
And I can always afford to share

You do not have to be rich
Or do bad things
It is all about you hugging all this love
That is growing in your heart
Never worry about being different
Work hard
Become a role model
Today is where you start
Discover how blessed you are
To be given all those crumbs
Because you most certainly discover
The more you learn to share
The more your life fills up with Crumbs!

My Jumper of Home

I have a jumper that fits me best
Woolly and soft
It puts my mind at rest
Anytime I feel a little afraid
It makes me smile
Like those funny tummy bubbles
In my glass of pop!
It snuggles in all those places
Whenever I feel far from home
It wraps me warm as toast
While chilly fills the day
Every stitch in its knitting
Gives me hugs
Out of all my jumpers
I love this one the most
It teaches me how to be strong
And I am simply perfect as I am
Never will I be far from love
Because my jumper is too long!

My jumper gives me confidence
Just when I am feeling a bit low
It tells me that I am never-ever alone
Then I can do important things
That make me feel important!
For I need help sometimes
If I could wear my jumper
Anytime I liked
There would be no sad or scary stuff
To make me be afraid
My jumper takes me Home

In these years of learning to grow
My big red jumper
Is the only other one that knows
How to calm and help me see
When my mind is lost
And I cannot see
All the good stuff in this world
There is a little label
Mum/Dad has sewn into the side
Addressed
'Return to sender!
To My Dearest Angel
Just return yourself to me whenever lost'

This tale explains how Love Is
To Give in the smallest ways
A day where you can make good
Whichever ways you wish to make a difference
For in this world of stuff and nonsense
We can shine our light of Being
There is nothing too small
In this scheme of life
You see
Abundance is in The Giving
Look up tonight at The Stars
And Shine Together
Jumper resting
Full of happiness
Ready for new adventures
To return you Home

Cake Contentment

In the time it takes to gather around our living room
The pastel-coloured mixer had mashed a batch of gloop
We shop at all the value stores
Cakes we believe are ancient friends
Archaeologists could discover our crumbed remains
We have a recipe we cannot divulge
In fear we cause a world-wide movement
Of sticky gunge and buttered stogies
Be responsible for
Kitchen alchemy
Where so few ingredients become necessary
Shopping will advance exponentially
Where people have no choice
Than to
Regress back to creating community
As my Girls know how to transform
Our busy-bodied weekends
Into the most relaxed and rested hours
Known to custard
And the very idea of being flustered
Is abhorrent to us three
Many hands-on-deck
The flurry of legs
A puff of flour from the chunky jars
We always use butter
Soft, squidgy and orangey-yellow

Our cakes are all baked
Smelly and soft
Always booked up for a date
With us of course!
Assortments of boxes
We used to use for our fruits and veg
Diversification our mind-therapy
Keeps us over the edge
But you know!
We would rather life this way
Normality has its place
In museums we say
Those sorts of places

Oddities of sockses
Though we found far too arty
For the bottom drawers
We know the power of cake
Life for us gives
Much more than it takes
We are all the richer
Though we still have little
In the big schemes of money
Life for us
Is so immensely Funny
And whatever you do
'Please do not underestimate
Eccentricities will become
A Piece of Cake!'

Giving is Infinite

Smallest pieces are enough
Where little needs suffice
Infinitesimal is to take
Only what is needed
In this less
There is more
I see them in my garden
When they know where my love awaits
They find my corners of offerings
It is beyond magic what they give
From that fragile bundle of innocence
To understand this world
Is to discover how to live
When a new dawn awakes
They find my corners of offerings
What they take has no comparing
To all they are
To all they give
In their visit they create such beauty
For their wish to live
With all they are
Bundles of love
That wish to give
They give their time
Then they will give much more
When you know
Just what miraculous is
They create a world
Full of miracles too
Then you discover
Just what has been allowed you.

Seriousness of Silly

Our wellies stood out in the rain
My girls and I agreed
We may as well leave them there
Lots of silly stuff you understand
It is far too important
To spoil a perfectly happy day
With overloads of serious things
That need immediate answers
Some things slow life down
Make you sad just for the fun of it
But we have worked life out
On some molecular level
That's our silly-summation
On this particular guff
Sounds quite scary I do agree
But we just work as one
Through problems of the day
Whatever comes our way
We have this covered
Like a happy child knows how to play
And we just do not have time
To lose the plot
Because at any given point
It is really all we got
When life comes down to the wire
We can call on our strengths
To work Together

Find where your heart is hidden
There really is no more time
To fool yourself or others
Face that demon in your head
It will not go away
Until you look it in the eye
Now where I am coming from
Underscores a need for happiness
Whether a short-lived whim
Or a design of your mind
To underestimate the power of happy
Will only lead to a life of grim and grind
Be the child that sees the truth
Be the ageless eyes of youth
Be the heart that beats
To the rhythm of universal life
Be the strength of a devoted parent
Be the giver to that lacking other
Be the fire burning in the bitter cold
Be the passion of an eternal friend
Be the beginning of an end
Of devastation
Be the drum of a nation's soul
Be the last part to complete the whole
Be the life without death
Be this fulfilled not the bereft
Be where your life is that place
Where nurturements are restored
Balance allowed to take its rightful place
Of that which has been lost
To our just creating happiness.

Wars of In-Humanity

One War
We all Fight

One World
We All Unite

One Life
Infinite Existences

One Thought
We All Create

One Choice
Infinite Journeys

One Hate
We Are All Destroyed

One Vision
Infinite Perceptions

One Loss
We All Suffer

One War
We All Die

One Strength
Infinite Wisdoms

One Understanding
We All Become Aware

One Consciousness
Infinite Enlightenments

One Integrity
We All Aspire

One Communication
Infinite Communities

One World
We All Nurture

One Wish
Infinite Consciousness

One Universe
We All Converge

One Soul
Infinite Sacredness*

Time to Grow

Wait a moment before you take things for granted
There is always someone so much worse off
Think a moment before eating your meal
There is always some place which suffers loss

Just a little place it can be happy
To help each other nurture
That green space in your garden
It does not need to be much or big
That will do lovely for any little thingamajig
Anything you can learn from a good soul
Listen to wise and clever friends
Between something they know
Something you know
Between you both
You will know more than enough
And it is all because you care
About What is important in this world
How looking after nature
Is not about having wealth
It is about nurturing Mother Nature
Giving little bits of your busy time
Learning what and how life is
Understanding where you can make
Sunshine in the pouring rain
So I agree!
This all sounds so insane
But you know!
Take a little moment to look around
See everything you can
Beautiful Things Will Grow

Please keep very still
Do not make a sound
Because it is not about
What life has to give you
That will happen in its own time
You will find it is about
What you have to give to life
Funny how this happens
In a world where it seems
Plenty comes
Plenty goes
Maybe this plenty is a place?
We do not really wish to be without
For some it is far too scary to find out
But all the same
It is not a game I wish to play
Not this day
Not Tomorrow anytime
Or anytime soon
Wait a moment before you eat your meal
Create a silent wish
Where you can make good things happen
Anytime you spend giving company
To your bestest friend
See how you can learn
To help this planet grow happy
The smallest thing
You can do to mend
Broken stuff

If you would keep your garden clean
Build lovely little safe corners
For nature's babies of our universe
Smallest of things will help
If you would give a moment of your day
Nothing is a waste of time
While you are giving
You are creating
What living is all about
You are so important
It is you this world needs
To help it grow
To help those who do not know
How simplicities make life so happy

One breath keeps us all alive
Where we can live for today
One breath keeps us all able to work
As one being upon this planet

One breath keeps us all with possibilities
To create important things upon this earth
One breath keeps us all in a world
Where everything is a choice
Our very being is a chance to make a difference

One breath keeps us all aligned
With a new world to nurture
One breath keeps us in the light
Our light of understandings
If we wish to give
When we give with everything we are

Universal Warriors

In the light
We can see all that has been illuminated
That which we wish to keep shadowed
Is of our choice
From that which remains within darkness
Shall be a source of all things most fearful
Our first spark of life
Where infinite miracles emerge
There in the knowing
In that knowing
Of something greater than all
I choose to walk within this light

There before
Here
There to come
There forevermore

And in this labyrinth of light
I choose to journey
To be at one
To absorb this love
With all I am
With all I can be
If here is where I learn
Of what life is meant to be
Until Then
Here is where I watch for angels

I wish you well upon your life's journeys
Though I never knew you
I was sent to set you free
Though you may never know me
We were always meant to be

I will not allow you any harm
Nor any dreams to lie unfulfilled
As my gift to you
Has come from other realms
Much longing to find you
And in as much,
As those who have no care
I will be forever watching over
I will be eternally protecting you there

Amidst lonely storms of loss
Within incessant piercing doubts
While some endeavours bleed
Upon your place of safety
I will be there
Somewhere
When you wish to hide
Far from the wolf of pain
Waiting with insatiable hunger
To devour your deepest fears

It is this storm
Without mercy or malintent
Is your saving grace
If only you look up
Your hour of need
Is a gate to your salvation
While merely walk on through,
Hold on to fears and phantoms
As when all demons rise
There comes a silence
Within such sacredness
You are become warrior

All that was
All that is
All that shall come forth

Is where hemispheres
Become aligned
Love awaits for all we are,
Strength is our shield,
Where we see with our soul,
Nurturement our armour,
Nevermore loss to walk as warriors

Are We Just a Dream?

I am a rock
That protects
All who wish to find refuge
I am a place of peace
Where nothing can harm you
I am a light
To guide your way
I am a window
To free your soul
I am fire
An eternal flame
Through darkest nights
I shall be here
I shall remain.
I am the day
That frees the sun
I hold this light
For it is you
That I have journeyed here
Now we shall shine together
I am that place
Where moon and sky
Paint magic upon the stars
Inside the minds
Of dreamers
So we can see a new day
As one mind

Dreams of Being

Being is something that transforms whatever it touches. You become it. It needs company. This is a new day, how about taking it for a walk. If you have a best friend that you can make time for. To be a good friend is one of the loveliest things in this whole, busy bee world. Whenever you feel that this world is too busy for you that day, just sit in a quiet place. Become quiet. Think things that you wish to keep you company for that moment. Happy things. Those things that are your best friends whenever you need them. They might have always been there. When you were a little child, they found you one day or night, and stayed with you because you both knew nothing would ever keep you apart in the whole of your busiest life.

And if it's fair to say, your whole world has been transformed by, and in, this universe of inexplicableness. To believe in something, anything that is not visible is to ask too much of almost anyone. Who in their right mind would believe in such things. Surely belief is as a certainty. A knowing of whatever has questioned your sanity is, for the better part, held in truth. Though you see, life will not give this certainty of credentials. It is up to us to prise apart the outer shell of uncertainty, teeth and all, delve in and pick up, examine, analyse and choose our diagnosis. Living within the orb of being is becoming your true self. Your integrity engages to its full potential. There is a peace.

The pages of days are turned by you. They have their own story. Their words are your deeds. Thought walks beneath a different light. Where life was as a distant place which required your compass to navigate the prevailing weathers of passing circumstances. Within being no external equipment is required. You are its captain, you its passenger, weather bears no powers in this dimension of the soul. You are the eye of the storms of experience, and so all that is lives within your experiences. It breathes through you. It is nurtured by you. It shall evolve from you. There is no beginning of this phenomenon of consciousness. It has always been. Empires rise. In the light of something fallen men of powers and pride have faded like ink upon ancient parchments. But for that time greatness flew as a phoenix, only to become the flames that would light the endless torches that lined those crumbling corridors of our past.

What of our past? That spectre of mind that lies silent inside jagged, abstract thoughts. Silence that screams at the broken windows of our perceptions. Echoes of its spirit haunt the abandoned castles of contentment and leave their fears to seed the cracks of our insecurities. In the here, within this breath of possibilities is a resurrection of our purpose, our perceptions. Dreams long held by the ether of our strengths. Dreams we dare dream, because they are that voice left amid the darkness of this earth's despair. To dream as a child is to nurture that which is innocence, that which returns us to our purpose.

Working with anything or anyone who lives without the affliction of ego, is where I live with knowledge of a oneness of my spirit. There is no substitute, it is alignment of my spirit with my soul. In the light of something. In becoming your dream, you then can dream your life.

Starfish

Starfish dreamt they could one day become stars, if they dreamt with all their heart together.

As they swam for such a long, long time in the deepest seas, they never stopped dreaming. Night after night they looked up at the skies and wished. Everything they did throughout each busy day held the silent words, words they did not need to speak as they all knew exactly what these words were and what they meant.

They all possessed highly evolved instincts. Instincts they had learnt to use as their own symbiotic language so long ago that even they had forgotten how long ago it was.

Stars shimmered back at the communities of starfish. They too had their own special language. It is the way of things, how communication happens. Sound is physical. Instinct something ethereal. Ethereal is that silent feeling you feel when no one else needs to speak or fills your mind with things they want to be filled with.

To cross these two worlds is to cross a bridge that cannot be seen. Cannot be heard, cannot be touched. Hence cannot be taken away. This language is not an earthly language. It can only be spoken within our being. It lives within our souls. Its powers can only come into being through the alchemy of nurturement. Nurturement is the food of which instinct grows. Nurturement is the food of which instinct thrives. Nurturement is the food of which instinct creates its bridge. This instinct can only then travel across this bridge. To the source of your being.

Starfish know that humans require plenty of help, support, understanding and love.
If you ever doubt, or feel alone, just look up into our darkest of nights, wish with all your heart.

Horizons of Completeness

In the event of life
Work with a friend
Share a little time
Create and always inspire
You never know what you can achieve!
After all
The course of life never runs smooth
But nothing can beat
Life with a forever friend
And as you know
Adjusting the ebb and flow
Alter your frame of mind
The right combination
Of common sense
And determination
It always seems so impressive
In someone else
My brain just is not wired that way
So you guessed it!
I stayed this way
With my quirks
And my colourful idiosyncrasies
My eccentricities
And my funny odd toes
From my love of all things sentient
To these charity clothes
I could not be anyone else
No matter what life brings

There is a kind of grace
When you make time stand still
In this heavy world of confusion
You make it fall into place
It is a state
Not a fate!
Powerful energies
That can correlate thoughts
And I recognise the fact
Not all endeavours
Intend to stay on track
And the hands of time
Keep turning clickety-clack!
But jump on board
There is always a place to find
It is not about where you are going
It is all about this journey!
So many possibilities
Lie in wait!
When you share your light
This world can see!
Those who find shoes
That they wish to walk in
Worn and torn
Sometimes left by the wayside
Walk gently onwards

Destinies of Orb

And so it was, Orb was now returned.

Where once dreams had been held by Guardians of the realm of dreams, reality has converged with sacredness itself. This is to be the age of all that is one with our universe and so, Orb's time has come.

A newest of days waited, feathered skies dressed in the most beautiful of warm colours. Rays of sunshine descended, like jewelled javelins thrown from ivory clouds, suspended within expanses of sapphire.

'There is work to be done!' Orb sang.

Her bed was such that it shone tiny star-lights onto the windows of all Etherialah, so as all would know when Orb was home. Time was how it is meant, after all those years in a dark and lonely place, hidden by ignorance.

While growing up in a home that was not a home. Unloved by a mother, who was not a mother, only for appearance's sake. Memories of that time are understood now. Orb has lived this desolation, lived its emptiness, lived through the infinite corridors of abandonment. So much longing for the father she was kept apart from. All those years where love was denied, from her, as well as her father. Cruelty inflicted within her mind, body, and spirit. Mostly for the thrill of the power. Often because there was nothing else to call upon, as motherhood was an alien concept, it required that sacred ingredient of nurturement's altruism, combined with integrity of spirit. Something so natural to some, it shines from every movement.

Alchemy of Orb's spirit, forces so unbalanced as to be evil, had been aligned by powers far beyond imagination.

These memories then were wounds she had learnt to repair, surviving from her warrior strengths. Strengths she believed were weaknesses. All the while giving beautiful grains of her being. Searching for a place to hide her spirit to keep it safe from the coldness of her daily life.

Whenever there was a moment that could offer happiness, it would be taken away, or destroyed in some way. Anything given by her father, had to be stolen away by spite. Wonderful presents would be torn away by threats and vindictiveness. Orb's father had to pay for his strength of spirit, happiness of heart, unyielding dedication to his daughter. The daughter he could only be a visitor to on occasions. So here, she carried this spirit within her safe place. There it shall always dwell, untouched, untouchable, sacredness itself. There cannot be a place for evil within such depth of love, such is this simplicity of sacredness. But for Orb such things were, and forever shall be held within her uniqueness of spirit. Her soul has become one with her true self at last. She is a protector of all that is. Her memories had now become her strengths, from these there could be no greater wisdom.

Light cascaded through her gossamer curtains. As warm rays surrounded her presence, a halo of shimmering mist appeared, as if summoned by some unseen force.

'Orb! Orb my daughter! Wake now, for the day has need of you. I am with you, my child, tell me what you wish, so that I may guide you.'

'Mother? I do not see you, where are you?'

'Here!' replied Earth. 'I am with your daughters; they need to know that you will be here with them for bedtime tonight.'

In this time of Orb's return, Captain of her guards,

Sword-maker Moon had become her completeness. These two daughters had been given from this sacredness of Etherialah, they are all and more of this sacred realm's dreams and wishes lived throughout these realms. The gifts, abilities of two such will combine the universe's sacredness into one sphere of perceptions, so that communication of all life will be as if language of the ether itself.

A sudden breeze ruffled Orb's braided plaits, that fell down her back like copper cables glinting in the morning rays, bridging the sky to the earthy colours of her cavernous bedroom.

'Good morning, Orb, beloved daughter of our Queen!'

Through the bronze beam of light suspended from the great stained-glass window, directly above Orb's bed, a familiar, silver silhouette flew gently down. Silence held the room transfixed by a magical feeling of anticipation.

'It is I, Tick-Tick, I have been chosen to be your teacher of all things sacred. Since you're returning to Etherialah I have designed many mind-orbs so you will understand which humans require your bridge of sacredness, so they are able to cross from their world into ours, if they so choose.'

As Tick-Tick floated towards Orb, another figure came into view. Female forms began materialising, winged, mercurial in form. There were four, then a central figure, taller, with metallic wings that pulsated with all unimaginable colours. Her four surrounding beings I will call angels as they filled Orb's mind with a completeness of consciousness and contentment that could only emanate from those who are sacredness itself.

'Orb! You know me well; I am your sister Ithean. Upon arrival you saw me too briefly, but we have all eternity to grow together. We have infinite worlds to nurture, infinitesimal hemispheres of existences to bring back together. We shall evolve our abilities to convergences far beyond that of greed, ignorance and destruction of this sacredness of all that is, returning to all that shall be. We are both sides of the bridge of hemispheres. In this endeavour, all that we are will be called into being. Everything and everyone here are in place for this shall be.'

Morning dressed the atmosphere with a majesty, guiding all and everything in a brightness of warmth. Trees glistened, forest floors were alive, emanating a force of protection as to create its nurturements upon every living being there. Nothing could be harmed, only a symbiotic reinvigoration was possible in this realm. The one supported the other, this was the all, and so it would be.

'You see my daughter, mother of my daughters of our new world, you see all that is, do you not?'

'I see all, my mother,' replied Orb. 'My sister gave me the bracelet of wisdom this day, I understand what we are, and so, what we shall be as one sphere.'

'With this bracelet our universe speaks through you, and thereon, through us. Later today you will take time with your brother Zein. Both your sister and he are to take you to meet our "stone of sacrean" centre of all that is inexplicable; but first, as Ithean has explained, time now for your merging within our worlds of nurturements. It will be in your knowing times of each and every day. It is for you then to discover all that is your realm.

'Here know, within your growing, you are the influence and force of nurturement you allow to be. Life given for us to be within its presence, is allowed to us. In this allowance, we evolve through its presence within our lives. Our nurturements are the gifts of sacredness we do then forge. As a sword is forged with the integrity of its maker, we

Etherians forge our beings with the sacredness that is our integrity. We allow ourselves to become this one sword of our combined, divine strengths.'

With that, the four guard angels closed around Earth as to highlight these profound words given to Orb. As Earth drew closer, she opened her arms, wrapped Orb within her being. Orb saw everything that was Etherialah in an instant. Her mother's wisdom was being overlaid upon Orb's memories. There was a thunderbolt that lit up the summer's morning so brightly it turned everything into silver upon all and everything, and there was silence.

As Earth began her departure towards the great oaken door, four guards had already lined the archway of its corridor. Their eyes were of rainbows; as Orb watched intently, she could see that they bore swords etched with strange writing upon them. When they moved their bodies, the swords became one with them.

'Make good your day of "oneness" my beloved daughter, I shall be with your daughters today, as is good for them to be at "oneness" with me. My granddaughters are forged from the most sacredness of our universes, they are eternity's evolvement. They are our destination beyond the bridge of infinity.'

'If you wish, Orb, come and join us at tonight's supper at the castle. We shall all be there. You will know when to arrive, Tick-Tick will be with you.'

'Yes, of course I shall be there with them,' Orb smiled.

'We will share stories together then. They always need to know we are always here for them whenever they need. They love to stay with you at any given time, Mother, you are a special kind of magic they also know is responsible for their mother, your child. They call you mama Earth and hug each other, as if you were there. When I ask, they tell me you are always with them.'

'Whenever they need you, you know of it,' replied Earth. 'Your orblings are from sacredness itself, all they do shall bring enlightenment into this universe. They cannot allow anything unbalanced into their existence. What they will achieve will allow a catalyst for karmic laws to be aligned. This bridge has now been brought into existence by you and your beloved Moon Sword-maker. We are grateful for beyond time for this miraculous forging of our genesis of enlightenment. Our genesis of hemispheres is now in alignment. Time itself is balancing that which has become undone.' Earth looked lovingly into Orb's eyes as she began her way toward her return to the main forge of the castle.

The oaken doors closed and Orb knew she was to get prepared for her day ahead. In the blink of an eye Bright Star had laid her clothes on the huge shell chair at the side of her shower.

'But I was about to call you for your help Star, how?'

'Remember? When we first met? Believe these wonderments of this, your home. All that is inexplicable is here and wherever you are,' whispered Star, 'just believe in what you are, and all will be.'

From there time carried Orb around and through incredible parts of her kingdom. Beings of the like she had never seen or ever known in her entire childhood. Even so, they felt so familiar. They lived in some quiet, quizzical corner of Orb's psyche. Whatever she encountered, whatever she experienced, it was as if she had always known of this wondrous unevenness, that had now metamorphosed into her native universe. Many hours passed, as if minutes, time had no restraints upon Etherialah. It would only time, as humans know it, as a means to tune in to humanity's sphere of existence. Time was a reference system for events, emotional crossroads, especially evolvement of individuality.

Deep orange, later morning, Tick-Tick looked over to Orb with a rather cheeky smile.

'How about we use a piece of time to sit a while, have a picnic, be with all?'

'Just what I was wishing, Tick-Tick.'

'Wasn't it!' he replied.

They looked at each other and laughed so loudly all the birds began laughing too. While Orb realised this magical moment, she smiled at Tick-Tick, and signed I love you over to him. She understood then and there, Tick-Tick was her childhood friend from when she had been in first school. Within this look, Tick-Tick understood her realisation of this bridge of memories, and they hugged and sat down under an enormous oak tree to unpack their scrumptious picnic Tick-Tick had prepared, with the help of some fabulous friends.

'Now we shall eat and rest a while, Orb. After, we need to go across the waterfall at the end of this forest, to the heart of "lake of eternities". Your moment to be with our "stone of memories". Here you will be completeness with our realm as a true warrior.'

Opening the picnic pod a small hummling flew out, rubbing its eyes, and yawned. The three looked-at each other with a knowing smile, then there was no holding back, they all laughed. Tick-Tick held out his hand and passed a beautiful, purple violet to the baby hummling. It giggled, then bowed graciously, popped the violet in a little backpack, laughing with a funny little buzzy sound, swaying to and fro.

'As you see, the hummlings gathered all the best morsels they knew you would love. Sweet Pea, who you have just met, has worked too hard and too early for such a little being,' illustrated Tick-Tick.

'Aw!' sighed Orb, 'a little girl! With such a strong spirit to nurture.'

Bowing gracefully, Tick-Tick sang, 'That is how Etherialah is to be! We all are nurturers for the good of all.'

'Will she be able to find her way home?' asked Orb.

'But of course!' chuckled Tick-Tick, 'every being here has a protection energy that keeps them safe and returns them to their families and friends in a heartbeat. Hummlings are wonderful souls, they are connectors of the art of communication. They come and go as they please, they can be anywhere and everywhere needed. Upon arrival at the castle, our hummlings will be there to make good all for our evening with your mother, father, sister, brother, and all our army that are to be spared time to celebrate your "completeness".

'Yes! Hummlings are our force of nature that are guardians for all our natures' beings. Telepathy is one of their abilities. Languages, they can translate anything. If it is unknown to all, they can analyse its origin and interpret its modern-day form of speak.'

'My word, Tick-Tick, is there nothing that is impossible here?'

'Nothing is not possible here, Orb,' laughed Tick-Tick, 'because nothing is nothing. Nothing has no substance worthy of being. Life is all-encompassing. Therefore, life gives without taking away. Life gives life!'

'It is a perpetuation of nurturement and regeneration. There is no undoing, no destruction, no desecration. When in life there is living. It is as simple as that!'

The food was of the juiciest, lovingly eaten, graciously appreciated, with the understanding of the work and nurturement lavished upon it to bring it to this moment in time. Such an adventure in such a short span of time, seemingly effortlessly, being in numerous places, with the greatest respect and gratefulness of their hallowed companies upon my chosen journey.

'Orb! When you touched our "stone of eternities" you were bestowed with our sacred knowledge of universal laws. But then you know this now, "Orb Ethereal".'

'I know this now, my dearest Tick-Tick.'

As the light began dimming, they knew it was time to head back across the forest to meet with Orb's family in its entirety.

It would be the first time Orb would have actually been able to spend any significant time with all her family. Although only a short span of time had passed in Etherialah, in human time many years had passed.

The forest was a beautiful and magical place. A place where those who live are with beautiful and magical powers. These powers create wondrous things, things so inexplicable no one from the outer world would understand where they are created and by whom. However, the outer world is but another hemisphere of our worlds. We are the guardians of hemispheres of this universe, this is why we are those who must nurture all life and allow instigations of sacredness, then protect all that is. But then you realise this to be how it is in Etherialah, soon after arriving.

For Orb, discovering more of the central forest was something beyond the explanations of words, beyond the human condition, far, far beyond physicality and the facades of existences.

It had just touched darkness. Tick-Tick smiled gently as he tapped his fabulous bracelet of many gems. 'Here we are Orb! This is one of the gateways to the "Castle of Etherialah".'

There stood an oak tree, one of the tallest Orb had ever seen. It went on up into the skies forever. Tick-Tick looked over to Orb and winked. Before Orb could wink back there was a warm feeling, as if being hugged by an old friend.

Enveloped in a purple light, Orb was now looking at a great silvered gate. The gate was already opening by an invisible force.

A familiar voice. 'Precisely on time, my daughter of gentility! Come with me, at last we can all be together this evening. Your daughters are up in the great library, they too will be hungry and ready for their suppertime! As they were being guided by Tick-Tick.'

'I am making my way over to our Queen. Your girls will laugh when they see me again, as they hid two pots of my honey, given by our sun bees this morning. They believed I had not noticed,' he added.

'That sounds like my babies,' chuckled Orb.

Queen Earth turned to Tick-Tick and winked. He returned the wink, then flew off in the direction of the main tower.

'So then, Orb, tell me all about your adventures through our heart forest, and keep your meeting with "stone of eternities" until after main supper, if you will.'

'There are so many infinite things here, Mother, my head is full of beauty.'

'How true my child, how true,' whispered Queen Earth.

Night began covering everything with shadows, time had arrived for Orb's supper of togetherness. All was in place, with splendour and abundance of love that shone out from the colours, the foods, the beautiful glasses and shelled plates that adorned the huge, hugeness of great hall's table. Throughout many and more moons Etherialah had seen so much incredibility for its loved beings. Diversity was the essential sacredness of the very air breathed. Where it was that some would be assigned certain tasks to take care of, of late, since *Orb's* return, those who wished to work on any particular tasks could and would help wherever they cared to. There were exceptions. Tick-Tick, along with the hummlings were given utmost freedom and their importance was without question.

This was not only here in Etherialah, but in all realms of our universe. It was they that guided the day-to-day running of each and all layers of Queen Earth's realms. It was they who gathered within Queen's counsel at ending of the seventh eve of sacredness. In human terms, this equated to the seventh evening of each week.

'*Orb* is upon arrival, my Queen!' hailed Tick-Tick.

Queen Earth signalled her guard to open the great oaken doors. As they did, there could be seen an endless corridor of warrior guards lined along the fire-flamed lit entrance to the great hall. Swords, silvered, glinted within orange glows that caught metals with their sparks of amber and garnets. The night air had filled with anticipation that whispered change long dreamt of, long remembered.

The deep sound of a ram's horn bellowed across the darkened forest, as if it was permeating up through the heart of Etherialah itself. All was silence. One of the warrior guards strode in with his sword across his chest, closely followed by *Orb*.

All eyes were upon the meet of their queen now reunited with her beloved daughter, for an official celebration. Queen Earth beckoned over to *Orb's* two daughters brought in from their nursery chambers. 'Here my daughter! Come sit beside your sister Ithean, she has so longed to reunite with you from when you had to leave our home. You would never have known this, but it has been Ithean who has been watching over your journeys every day, so I would know how life was for you in the earth realm. We could not show ourselves in any way, while you were growing up there. But knowing you as I do, I suspect that your instincts are far too powerful to be shrouded in any way by the mind curtains of the human condition and the world thereof.'

In the blink of an eye, both sisters were united as both sides of the Orb of sacredness. Time had arrived to bring oneness of all realms. It required each and every being to work in harmony, for the good of all.

Cardigan and Me

Woolly and warm
Bright
As big buttons adorn
Your cuddliness
When I play chess
With my friends
I have huge pocket
To hold all my chocolates
It is all about sharing
My friends and I
Are not one for caring
About keeping things for ourselves
Whatever we have
Nothing makes us happier
Than finding ways
To create great days
Come evening we can snuggle home
With this lovely feeling
Of how we can make good things happen
Tomorrow needs our help
My cardigan is a friend to me
Whatever day it is always
Ready and waiting just to be
And all those days
I need the biggest hugs
It cuddles me up
And I feel like
A very clever bug
In the snuggliest rug!
That's my cardigan and me

So soon I wish to be home
There worlds collide
And nothing
But, nothing
Dismantles my soul
Nor solitude of heart
I fly amongst the stars
To wish to journey
Endless realms
As all us gentle souls
And look unto our universe
Then to know all we see
Is magical

So here I sit in contentment
Just my cardigan and me
Wild winds when out to play
Chilly ears
Peeking through
Chunky knit hats
Sweet sticky fingers
Pausing to eat a chocolate
Or two!
When weekend finds us
We always have time to spare
We just grab our coats
Without a doubt
We all arrive together!
Adored and adorned with a whole world of cardigans
From those who love us beyond words
It is where each stitch is knitted
Every loving stitch will carry
Love keeps us warm
Where Cardigan goes

Author's Note 2

Here the genesis of **Orb's** ethereal universe, with her eternal families of warriors, wonderments and wishes, as we have now come to realise all these magical beings are in the loving care of our Tick-Tick, unmistakably their invaluable guardian. While incredibility of Etherialah ebbs and flows, within depths far, far beyond dreams and imaginations humans dare dream. But some of us do. We create bridges from this world of impermanence, through impossibility, securing it to worlds of incredibility, from our incandescence of infinitesimal spirits. We then allow all that is sacredness, our choice defines us.

Queen Earth's gentility, which creates the nurturing foundations of Etherialah, is the constant aura of individuality, the very colours of sacredness, source of such a magical frequency. Each soul has an integral part to play throughout Etherialah's jewelled tapestry, festooning minds, and hearts with the most beautiful of intentions, along with life devotion, integrity of wisdom, in essence, their combined powers of uniqueness. Were it not for such a unification of mind and soul, these inexplicable ways of being would not be in the realms of consciousness, hence possible, not to mention dreamt.

To dream is to be a child. To travel beyond subconsciousness, is to be as innocence, the child. Innocence of the child transforming dreams into wishes, that become a complete sphere of convergence of love. Communities, with wills of warriors, their children grown from a world of nature's clarity. Bright lights that fill our souls with their healing. Bright lights that nurture our hearts with their purity. Bright lights that float like fireflies throughout our universe as orbs of illumination.

Only you, as the reader, know whether the contents of this book have resonated in any way, shape or form within your psyche. These are truly strange and wondrous journeys. I admit to the unmistakable fact, that they have been forged from an even stranger chemistry of something truly remarkable. They strangely bear an indelible mark that has been created through a combination of some of the alchemies.

As explained, language alone cannot translate inexplicableness. It is, as you have no doubt found, communication of the senses. An innate choice of interactions of integrity. An allowance of one's base instincts, acceptance of your soul's absolution, or self-belief within your sphere of awareness, that is absolutely yours to endeavour to translate. Such a mark is seared into one's soul, with a 'signature of sacredness', impossible to replicate from earthly elements.

Here in the realms of Orb, I have no need to apologise for her mind landscape. Those of you who have come to choose to be a passenger of her vehicle of discovery, are now returned and shall be my much-loved companions, that inspire these infinitesimal seeds of creativity to continue to allow themselves to seek out wondrous futility of our human minds, so they, in turn, will wish to grow and unfurl their sacred consciousness, to nurture all and more of this world we have been allowed. Here is where I choose. I choose to nurture this inexplicable being, that has created all and every oddity about me.

I choose and am humbled to be allowed its nurturement.

I choose how I can sculpt its form and its futility of emotions. This has been allowed me for a reason

For me, our existence has not been mere chance, a quirk of chemistry, an inevitability of science, brought about through perfectly timed forces of nature. These are my beliefs, as all beliefs are one's own choice. At the centre of beliefs, something inexplicable dwells. Whatever one's lifestyle, whatever one's belief, we allow ourselves to become part of, to disassemble our psyche, to resurrect some part of us which binds us together.

Our consuming need to belong to something greater than that which we perceive to be our life's Belonging, therefore, is of our giving. For the greater good of ourselves, we are needed, by our biodiversity, our diversity, our gifts of creativity, we choose to nurture from our incomprehensible creation.

We are then that essential force of nature, by our very existence, who are earth's guardians. Our wealth is abundantly clear, we are Universe.

My dream is that Orb becomes a bridge across this world's consciousness, into your individual hemispheres of existence. As you have become part of this book's journeys within its pages, this book will then resonate with yours. I wish you safe passage throughout this universe.

May your wisdom become your enlightenment. As you choose your paths, may you walk through this beauty, you have the power, through choice, to create within your light of consciousness.

Namaste*

Aurora of Spirit

Incandescence's colour spirit
Drumming each pulse of your heart
Skies descend
Watched over
By a universe of darkness
Awaiting its sacredness of light
With child of infinite
To be born
In this becoming.
Our galaxies unite
There we enter all
And in this become
We carry its light
It is choice
Where deeds are sown
There is a knowing
What is to be
If we align our atoms
Within wishing heart and breath
Our journey will find us
Silence amid our hallowed sky
Of I that shall hold this light
Within me
For all will no more be lost
As we then are Immortal
Whereupon once was lost
Reach out your spirit

Live today with everything and more
Let it become beauty
Waited more than time itself
My wish to merge unto these colours
That shall heal this world
Where life can live
Where we grow worlds
Where legends are our legacies
And earthly time can converge
Incandescence's return emerging
Become dreams
Of impossibilities
Allow these gates of inexplicabilities
Open upon our gaze
Allow our dreams
To find our gentle place
We are One!
Amid our seas of dreams
Where we can walk barefoot
Through all our possibilities
We will speak as One
Across our hemispheres
Across this sacred universe
For you who dream impossibilities
Choose to nurture life
All that is love
Become Your Universe
To All That IS.

Namaste.